NEW CLASSICS

NEW CLASSICS
MARCUS WAREING

with Chantelle Nicholson

Photography by
Jonathan Gregson

HarperCollins*Publishers*

NOTES ON INGREDIENTS

Unless otherwise stated:

Use large free-range eggs

Use whole milk (but semi-skimmed can be substituted, if you like)

Use unsalted butter

Use standard plain flour

Use fresh herbs (1 bunch = 25g)

Use medium-sized fruit and vegetables

HarperCollins*Publishers*
1 London Bridge Street
London SE1 9GF

www.harpercollins.co.uk

First published by HarperCollins*Publishers* 2017

Text © Marcus Wareing 2017
Photography © Jonathan Gregson 2017

10 9 8 7 6 5 4 3 2 1

A catalogue record of this book is available from the British Library.

ISBN 978-0-00-824273-2

Prop stylist: Jo Harris
Food stylist: Marina Filippelli
Assistant food stylist: Becks Wilkinson

Printed and bound by GPS Group

MIX
Paper from
responsible sources
FSC™ C007454

This book is produced from independently certified FSC paper to ensure responsible forest management.
For more information visit: www.harpercollins.co.uk/green

CONTENTS

INTRODUCTION

What does the phrase 'new classic' mean when discussing food? To me, when talking of a 'classic' in cookery, I think of tradition, dishes that are tried and tested, or that represent a time or place, and have stood the test of time. The notion of a 'new classic' accepts that a shift has taken place, whether in taste, produce or technique, which means a new twist can be put on that dish. I want to share these recipes with you, to introduce you to new flavour combinations and cookery methods that you may not have used before. I also want to reveal my favourite dishes that are in the process of becoming classics – brilliant dishes that will become time-honoured themselves.

The 'classics' were exactly what I learnt at college in the 1980s. Dishes such as lobster Thermidor, sole bonne femme, béarnaise, lemon meringue pie, millefeuille, éclairs, croissants – the list goes on and on. The techniques involved in these recipes, such as emulsifying, braising, sauce-making and pastry skills, were the cornerstones of my training. Most of you will be familiar with a number of these dishes and would deem them as 'classics', but I would hazard a guess that you cook and eat them very rarely – some because of their heaviness or the lengthy work involved, and some just because they're not to our modern tastes. This is what led me to write this book. I felt that, while classics will always have a firm place in any cuisine, new versions of the classics and new classics themselves deserve to come to the fore.

When I was a child, our family ate relatively simple food – generally meat and two veg, one of which was almost always a potato. As a family, we were not particularly adventurous and my siblings and I ate what was put in front of us. We all sat down together as a family to have our evening meal, though – always. My favourite dinner was roast leg of lamb with mint sauce and Jersey royals, followed by apple pie and cream. Fast-forward to today, and what my wife and children and I eat together is much more varied. We've always encouraged our children, and still do, to try new foods and flavours. These days you're likely to find us eating chicken curry on a weeknight, and enjoy a pork chop with mustard sauce and tarragon on a Sunday. My children are very keen cooks themselves, which is of course actively encouraged!

Any good dish must start with great ingredients. It was in my father's fruit and potato warehouse that I learnt the value of ingredients. I began to understand the difference between the flavour of unripe fruit and that of wonderfully vibrant, ripe produce. Selecting seasonal ingredients will ensure they are at their best. As I have always advocated in my cooking, ingredients are a key factor to success, so I have divided up the recipes by where we source our ingredients: the garden, the farm, the sea and the storecupboard.

FROM THE GARDEN

This chapter is something close to my heart – my father is the one to thank for my love of the humble vegetable. When sourcing ingredients, ripeness is key. Do not be afraid of over-ripeness, as this can often intensify flavour and sweetness. The Summer Vegetable Lasagne (page 60) is my take on a great recipe for families, as it is a delicious way to get children to enjoy vegetables. Another favourite is Tempura Fennel (page 36), a flavoursome dish that allows the fennel to really sing out. If you want to try making your own ravioli, I've provided a twist on the classic with my Mushroom 'Ravioli' with Shallot Sauce (page 42). In this chapter I also look in-depth at the technique of salt-baking (page 31). By making a salt dough and infusing it with herbs, you can impart seasoning and flavour deep into vegetables, as well as meat and fish. It is a great, simple technique that adds so much to any dish, so why not try it with the Salt-baked Parsnip and Horseradish Crumble (page 32) for a winter supper or the Salt-baked Kabocha Squash, Pomegranate, Ricotta and Mint (page 35) in late summer?

FROM THE FARM

Here I feature some of my favourite cuts of meat, such as Hanger Steak (page 81), which is rather underused. There is also my favourite Roast Chicken recipe (page 78), where the chicken is baked with fennel and potatoes. Both recipes showcase brining (page 77), which seasons meat or fish right to the core and tenderises it in the process. It takes a little more organisation but it's well worth it, with a tender, moist and well-flavoured dish as a result. The caramelised pears give an extra dimension to a classic Slow-cooked Pork Belly (page 112) for a weekend family lunch, and my Herb and Mozzarella Meatball Bake (page 138) is a great one for a midweek supper. When it comes to meat, look for good marbling in beef and lamb and vibrant flesh. What the animals are fed on can also affect the flavour and texture of the meat, so if you can, buy grass-fed or pasture-fed.

FROM THE SEA

This takes me back to my time at the Savoy Hotel kitchen when I was 17 and working on the fish section. I have included a few classics, such as Fish Soup (page 154), which I've updated with a few of my own ideas, while eggy bread is given a delicious makeover in Prawn French Toast (page 162). In this chapter I also feature the technique of hot smoking (page 165). Traditionally this is done to preserve fish, but more importantly for us it adds another flavour dimension to the dish. Smoke is a match made in heaven with oily mackerel, so look for my recipe for Rosemary Smoked Mackerel with Baked Lemon Jam, Fennel and Crème Fraîche (page 166). You might be used to smoked salmon, eggs and hollandaise for brunch, but once you've tried it with home-smoked salmon in my twist-on-a-classic Hot Smoked Salmon Eggs Benedict (page 168), you won't go back. For fish and seafood, choose the brightest-looking fish, with no strong smells. When purchasing seafood, always look for the glossiest produce and wash well in cold water before using.

FROM THE STORECUPBOARD

This chapter encompasses baking recipes that use base ingredients potentially already in your cupboard (which makes baking possible when you have last-minute cravings!). As well as cakes, biscuits and tarts, there are breads such as Marmite, Onion and Cheddar Bread (page 248), which is a favourite with my kids and a lovely accompaniment to soup. When it comes to puddings, you can't beat the Baked Honeycomb Puddings (page 230) as a delicious finish to a Sunday lunch. I also focus on caramelising sugar (page 235), something which can seem a little daunting. It's not a complicated method once you know how; the trick is to be patient and ready for the next step as soon as the sugar begins to colour. Try out the technique with one of my favourites in this chapter, the Warm Spiced Courgette Cake with Anise Caramel (page 238), which is a lovely pale green at the centre – it's a good way to get a few more vegetables into children and for them to see the versatility of ingredients. Caramel finds its way into ice cream as well, here, for a delicious pudding of Banana and Coconut Cake with Caramelised Banana Coconut Ice Cream (page 236).

Above all, do remember to enjoy cooking. Food is something to be treasured, and cooking is such a wonderful way to learn, educate, socialise and enjoy quality time with family and friends. So please don't be daunted by any of these recipes – they have all been written with home cooking in mind. This book is about sharing my passion for cooking and ingredients with all kinds of home cooks, from beginners all the way up. My advice is to dive straight in! Enjoy reading, creating and, of course, eating.

FROM THE GARDEN

Apple and cheese is a classic combination, and my twist on a refreshing summer salad is to pair watermelon and savoury salted ricotta. Instead of discarding watermelon rind, try pickling it. It has a great texture and keeps for quite some time in the fridge. It works well as an accompaniment to most meat and fish, and in salads, like this one.

WATERMELON WITH PICKLED RIND, SALTED RICOTTA AND CORIANDER SALAD

Peel the green layer off the watermelon, then remove the pink flesh from the white rind (put the pink flesh in a bowl, cover and chill) and carefully slice the white rind into roughly 1cm chunks. Put all the pickle ingredients in a small saucepan and bring to the boil. Add the chunks of watermelon rind and bring back up to the boil. Remove from the heat and allow to steep for 30 minutes. Cover and chill for at least 24 hours.

Cut the pink watermelon flesh into roughly 1.5cm cubes, removing as many black and white seeds as you can (with a skewer). Mix the olive oil and lime zest and juice together in a bowl. Season the watermelon with sea salt and pepper and dress it with the oil and lime.

Divide the watermelon flesh between four plates. Drain off the pickled watermelon rind and add it to the plates. Finely grate the salted ricotta over the top of the watermelon (use a Microplane grater for this if you have one) then finish with the coriander leaves.

Serves: 4

Preparation time: 15 minutes, plus minimum 24 hours pickling

½ watermelon (approximtely 1.2kg)
4 tbsp olive oil
grated zest and juice of 1 lime
50g salted ricotta cheese
¼ bunch of coriander, leaves picked
sea salt and freshly ground black pepper

FOR THE PICKLE
100ml white wine vinegar
4 tbsp runny honey
6 whole white peppercorns
2 cloves
1 bay leaf
1cm piece of fresh ginger, peeled and sliced
½ tsp yellow mustard seeds
½ tsp table salt

This is a great salad for when the weather starts to turn cooler. Kale has a rather robust texture which lends itself well to being eaten either raw or cooked. In this recipe I have included both: the raw kale adds a freshness to the salad and the fried kale adds a light smokiness to the overall flavour.

KALE, TOASTED ALMOND AND FRIED SAGE SALAD

Heat half of the vegetable oil in a large frying pan over high heat. When hot, add the shallots, season well with sea salt and cook for 6–8 minutes, until golden. Add half the kale and cook for a further 2 minutes until it just begins to wilt, then transfer the kale and shallots to a bowl.

Heat the remaining oil in a medium frying pan. When hot, add some of the sage leaves and fry for 2–3 minutes over high heat until crispy (fry them in batches). Place on kitchen paper to soak up the excess oil and season well with sea salt.

When the sage leaves have been fried, add the flaked almonds to the pan, season with sea salt and toast until golden. Remove from the heat.

To make the dressing, mix all the ingredients together in a bowl.

Thinly slice the remaining raw kale and mix it together in the bowl with the cooked kale, shallots, almonds and fried sage leaves. Season with more sea salt and loads of black pepper and drizzle with the dressing.

Serves: 4
Preparation time: 10 minutes
Cooking time: 20 minutes

2 tbsp vegetable oil
2 shallots, thinly sliced
500g kale, tough stems removed
½ bunch of sage, leaves picked
100g flaked almonds
sea salt and freshly ground black
    pepper

FOR THE DRESSING
3 tbsp balsamic vinegar
1 tsp wholegrain mustard
125ml olive oil
1 garlic clove, finely grated

Nothing beats a plate of tomatoes dressed in olive oil as a late-summer starter. Here I add goats' cheese and my favourite black olives, Kalamata, for a real depth of flavour with the sweetness of tomatoes and shallots. Tomatoes taste much sweeter when they are at room temperature, rather than fridge-cold. They will also ripen quicker stored outside the fridge.

TOMATO, GOATS' CHEESE AND BLACK OLIVE SALAD

Whisk the oil and balsamic vinegar together in a bowl. Add the capers and shallots and set aside to marinate for 20 minutes.

Generously season the tomatoes with salt and pepper and arrange them on a serving plate. Dress them with the dressing then crumble the goats' cheese on top. Finish with the olives and lightly tear the basil leaves to scatter on top. Serve immediately.

Serves: 4
Preparation time: 15 minutes, plus
    20 minutes marinating

4 tbsp extra virgin olive oil
1 tbsp good-quality balsamic vinegar
1 tsp capers in brine, strained and
    finely chopped
2 shallots, finely sliced
4 ripe plum tomatoes, sliced
8 ripe baby plum tomatoes, halved
120g soft goats' cheese
50g pitted Kalamata olives, chopped
¼ bunch of basil
sea salt and freshly ground black
    pepper

I love the earthiness of Jerusalem artichokes. They are also a great staple during the winter months and right at the beginning of spring when everything is still a little sparse. Give them a good scrub to remove any grit or dirt, instead of peeling them before cooking, as the skin is very flavoursome.

ROASTED JERUSALEM ARTICHOKES WITH CONFIT LEMON AND A GARLIC AND PICKLED WALNUT DRESSING

Preheat the oven to 220°C/200°C fan/gas 7.

Place the washed artichokes, 2 tablespoons of vegetable oil, butter and thyme in a roasting tray, toss to coat the artichokes in the oil, and season with salt and pepper. Cut the tops off the garlic bulbs, place them in foil, drizzle them with the remaining 1 tablespoon of vegetable oil and season with sea salt. Fold the foil over to enclose the garlic bulbs and place them in the roasting tray with the Jerusalem artichokes. Bake for 30–40 minutes, depending on the size of the artichokes, stirring every 10 minutes, until the artichokes are dark golden, the centres are soft and the garlic is soft and golden. Remove from the oven and allow to cool slightly, then cut the artichokes in half and place them back in the roasting tray to keep warm, adding a little more salt and pepper.

Allow the garlic to cool slightly then squeeze the flesh out of the bulbs and set aside.

While the artichokes are baking, make the confit lemon. Cut the lemon in half lengthways, removing the seeds, then slice it finely. Place in a saucepan with the sugar and thyme and cover with 100ml water. Place over low heat, bring to a simmer and cook for 20–30 minutes until the lemons are soft. You may need to add a little more water if it evaporates too quickly. Remove the thyme stalks and set aside.

Mix the roasted garlic flesh in a bowl with the chopped pickled walnuts, olive oil and pickling liquor and season to taste.

Arrange the artichokes on a large serving platter, using all of the roasting juices too. Top with the confit lemon and the walnut dressing.

Serves: 6
Preparation time: 15 minutes
Cooking time: 40 minutes

2kg Jerusalem artichokes, scrubbed clean
3 tbsp vegetable oil
25g butter
¼ bunch of thyme
2 garlic bulbs
sea salt and freshly ground black pepper

FOR THE CONFIT LEMON
1 lemon
2 tbsp caster sugar
¼ bunch of thyme

FOR THE WALNUT DRESSING
3 tbsp chopped pickled walnuts
4 tbsp olive oil
1 tsp pickled walnut pickling liquor

This is my spin on a classic vegetable soup. If you are feeling a little under the weather, or in need of a bit of goodness, then this is the ticket. You can add any other vegetables you have in your fridge, too – the more the merrier. The dumplings are very easy to make and can also be used to serve with pasta and homemade tomato sauce.

SUPER-GREEN SOUP
WITH RICOTTA DUMPLINGS

To make the ricotta dumplings, beat the ricotta in a bowl with the lemon zest and a pinch of sea salt and pepper. Roll the mixture into 16 balls then roll the balls in the semolina until thoroughly coated. Transfer to a plate and chill for 1 hour to firm up.

Heat the 2 tablespoons of vegetable oil in a large saucepan over medium heat. Add the onion, bay leaves and table salt. Cook for 7–10 minutes until the onion is soft but not coloured. Add the vegetable stock and simmer gently for 20 minutes.

While the stock is simmering, cook the dumplings. Lightly grease a steamer with oil and arrange the ricotta dumplings inside. Set the steamer above a pan of simmering water, cover and steam for 5 minutes. (You may need to do this in batches, depending on the size of your steamer.)

Remove the bay leaves from the saucepan and add the leek. Simmer for 5 minutes, then add the broccoli. Simmer for 3 minutes then finish with the spinach leaves and chopped herbs. Taste and adjust seasoning if necessary.

Add a few dumplings to each bowl of soup, sprinkle with black pepper and finish with a drizzle of olive oil.

Serves: 4
Preparation time: 20 minutes, plus
    1 hour chilling
Cooking time: around 40 minutes

2 tbsp vegetable oil, plus extra for
    greasing
1 onion, sliced
2 bay leaves
½ tsp table salt
800ml–1 litre Vegetable Stock
    (page 57)
1 leek, finely sliced (white part only)
1 broccoli head, finely chopped
100g baby spinach leaves
1 tbsp finely chopped tarragon
1 tbsp finely chopped flat-leaf parsley
extra virgin olive oil, for drizzling
sea salt and freshly ground black
    pepper

FOR THE RICOTTA DUMPLINGS
240g ricotta cheese
grated zest of ½ lemon
4 tbsp semolina

I have always loved a good soup and this is one of my most recent favourites. Celeriac is a great winter vegetable with an interesting, almost menthol, flavour that pairs very well with the sweetness of apple and the smokiness of the crème fraîche. Celeriac is in season from autumn right through to the end of winter.

CELERIAC AND APPLE SOUP WITH SMOKED CRÈME FRAÎCHE

Melt the butter in a large saucepan over medium heat. When hot, add the celeriac, onion, table salt and bay leaves and cook for 7–10 minutes, until soft but not browned. Add the diced apple and vegetable stock and simmer gently for 20 minutes. Add the milk then remove the pan from the heat, remove the bay leaves and blend in a blender until smooth. Pass through a fine sieve into a clean saucepan and season with sea salt and pepper to taste.

Smoke the crème fraîche according to the method on page 165, spreading it as thinly as possible in a foil dish and putting the dish on the smoking rack. Once smoked, remove the tray and set aside for 10 minutes. Remove the foil then scrape the crème fraîche into a bowl and whisk to evenly distribute the smokiness. Season with a little sea salt.

To serve, finely julienne the remaining apple, with the skin on, and mix it in a bowl with the sesame oil, seasoning it with sea salt and pepper to taste.

Serve the soup in bowls, topped with a good dollop of the smoked crème fraîche and the julienned apple.

Serves: 4
Preparation time: 20 minutes
Cooking time: around 30 minutes

25g butter
1 celeriac (around 500g), peeled and
    cut into 1.5cm chunks
1 onion, sliced
½ tsp table salt
2 bay leaves
2 Granny Smith apples, 1 peeled
    and diced
600ml Vegetable Stock (page 57)
300ml milk
1 tbsp toasted sesame oil
sea salt and freshly ground black
    pepper

FOR THE SMOKED CRÈME
FRAÎCHE
1 x quantity of Smoke Mix (page 165),
    using 1 tbsp black tea leaves
100g crème fraîche

Think of a hot summer's day when it comes to this soup. It really does hit the spot, and being vegan and gluten-free, it is a good recipe to make if you are having guests over who may have food intolerances. The cobs of corn have a sweet flavour, too, so do not throw them away. Use them to flavour soups and stocks.

CHILLED SWEETCORN SOUP WITH AVOCADO SALSA, CHILLI AND BLACK SESAME SEEDS

Heat 2 tablespoons of the vegetable oil in a large saucepan over medium heat. When hot, add the cobs of corn and fry them for 5–7 minutes. When golden, add the vegetable stock, bring to the boil, then reduce the heat and simmer for 20 minutes.

Remove the cobs from the stock and add three-quarters of the sweetcorn kernels and the table salt. Cook for 10 minutes, or until the kernels are soft.

Remove from the heat, add the coconut milk and blitz the soup in a blender or using a stick blender, until smooth. Season to taste (if necessary) then chill.

Heat the remaining tablespoon of vegetable oil in a medium frying pan. When hot, add the remaining sweetcorn kernels and cook for 4–5 minutes until soft. Remove from the heat and leave to cool.

Combine the chilli, lime zest and juice, coriander, sesame oil and sesame seeds in a bowl and season with sea salt. Gently fold through the diced avocado.

Divide the chilled soup between four bowls and garnish with the whole sweetcorn kernels and dressed avocado.

Serves: 4
Preparation time: 15 minutes
Cooking time: 40 minutes,
    plus chilling

3 tbsp vegetable oil
4 cobs of corn, kernels sliced off
    and husks retained
800ml Vegetable Stock (page 57)
½ tsp table salt
100ml coconut milk
sea salt and freshly ground black
    pepper

FOR THE AVOCADO SALSA
1 green chilli, deseeded and
    finely chopped
grated zest and juice of 1 lime
1 tbsp chopped coriander
2 tbsp toasted sesame oil
2 tbsp black sesame seeds
1 ripe avocado, halved, peeled,
    stoned and diced

Burrata is one of my all-time favourite cheeses and makes a stunning starter. It is quite unlike any other cheese, with a mozzarella shell filled with creamy stracciatella. It used to be very difficult to get hold of, but it is now available from cheesemongers and some larger supermarkets (buy the best mozzarella you can find if not).

BURRATA WITH ROMESCO SAUCE AND GRILLED PADRON PEPPERS

To make the romesco sauce, place all of the ingredients in a food processor and pulse until you have a chunky paste. Season with sea salt and black pepper. Divide between four plates.

Heat a dry grill pan over high heat until smoking. Drizzle the padron peppers with a little oil and seasoning, then grill for about 5 minutes until lightly blackened.

If using small burrata balls, tear them over the romesco. If you're using larger burrata, cut them almost all the way through then peel open and add half a burrata per portion, cut side facing up, to the romesco. Drizzle with olive oil and season well. Garnish with the grilled padron peppers and serve immediately.

Serves: 4 as a starter
Preparation time: 15 minutes
Cooking time: 5 minutes

12 fresh padron peppers (approx. 60g in total)
splash of vegetable oil
4 x 100g or 2 x 200g balls burrata
1 tbsp extra virgin olive oil

FOR THE ROMESCO SAUCE
100g roasted red peppers, deseeded and skin removed, or piquillo peppers (from a jar or tin), drained and roughly chopped
50g flaked toasted almonds
3 tbsp olive oil
½ tsp sweet smoked paprika
2 tbsp chopped flat-leaf parsley
2 tsp tomato purée
splash of dry sherry
sea salt and freshly ground black pepper

A great alternative to a traditional cheese board, this baked feta combines salty cheese with fragrant, lightly caramelised honey. Serve with these crisp rye bread crackers, crusty bread or your favourite cheese biscuits. I love the fragrant lavender in this dish – it really adds a point of difference.

HONEY-BAKED FETA WITH LAVENDER, THYME AND RYE CRISPS

Preheat the oven to 200°C/180°C fan/gas 6.

Cover the feta with 2 pieces of kitchen paper and leave at room temperature for 1 hour to absorb excess moisture.

Cut the rye bread into very thin slices. Place them in a single layer on 2 baking trays. Drizzle with the olive oil and rub each slice with a halved garlic clove.

Bake the rye slices in the oven for 7–10 minutes until lightly golden and crisp. Remove the rye crisps and turn the oven to its grill setting.

Remove the kitchen paper from the feta and place the feta in an ovenproof dish just large enough for it to fit in snugly. Drizzle the honey on top, then add the thyme and lavender. Season well with sea salt and pepper and grill for 5–10 minutes until golden.

Remove the cheese from the grill. Serve the feta immediately with the rye crisps.

Serves: 4
Preparation time: 10 minutes, plus 1 hour draining
Cooking time: 12–20 minutes

1 x 200g block feta cheese
½ loaf rye bread
4 tbsp olive oil
1 garlic clove, halved
3–4 tbsp runny honey
4 sprigs of thyme
2 sprigs of fresh lavender or ½ tsp dried lavender
sea salt and freshly ground black pepper

Courgette flowers are another of those wondrous ingredients that signal the arrival of warmer weather. Not much needs doing to them as they are perfect simply fried in a little oil and served with this sauce. Choose the flowers that are large and firm, as they can accommodate more stuffing and will retain their shape better when cooked.

COURGETTE FLOWERS WITH RICOTTA AND SWEET BASIL SAUCE

Mix the ricotta with the lemon zest and season with sea salt and pepper to taste. Fill each courgette flower with the mix and chill while you make the batter (you can stuff them up to 2 hours ahead of time, if you wish).

To make the tempura batter, mix the cornflour and flour together in a bowl. Gradually whisk in enough of the soda water to make a thick batter. Season with a pinch of sea salt.

To make the sweet basil sauce, place all the ingredients in a small food processor and blend until smooth.

To fry the flowers, pour enough vegetable oil in a deep-fat fryer or large, deep saucepan to come up to 4–6cm and heat it to 180°C.

Dust two of the courgette flowers in flour, dip them in the batter, then carefully place them in the hot oil. Fry for 4–6 minutes until deep golden and crisp. Remove each flower with a large slotted spoon and transfer to kitchen paper to remove any excess oil, then season with sea salt if needed. Repeat with the remaining two flowers.

Serve immediately with the basil sauce.

Serves: 4 as a starter

100g ricotta cheese
grated zest of ½ lemon
4 courgette flowers
vegetable oil, for deep-frying
sea salt and freshly ground black
    pepper

FOR THE TEMPURA BATTER
6 tbsp cornflour
3 tbsp plain flour, plus extra for dusting
3–6 tbsp soda water

FOR THE SWEET BASIL SAUCE
1 bunch of basil, leaves only
juice of 1 lemon
4 tbsp olive oil
1 tbsp drained, chopped capers in brine
1 tbsp runny honey

SALT-BAKING

As a chef, and for any home cook, salt can transform a dish from bland to flavoursome.

I prefer to create a salt dough, rather than use a crust of salt alone, as you can add different ingredients to the dough which then impart even more flavour to the food it encloses. The flour in the dough also lessens the intensity of the salt, enabling more control over the seasoning. Salt-baking works in two ways: firstly, the dough creates a shell for the food, trapping in the heat during cooking so the juices are retained and the food is steamed within the crust. Secondly, it seasons the food while it's cooking, with the salt permeating throughout. Traditionally salt-baking has been used to cook meat, fish and poultry (and you'll find a Salt-baked Shoulder of Lamb on page 132). I'm focusing here on salt-baked vegetables to highlight what a brilliant technique it is for bringing out their wonderful flavour.

For salt-baking, rock salt is the only salt to use. Unlike sea salt and table salt, it retains its texture, so the food you are cooking will not be over-seasoned. I mix the salt with plain white flour (which can easily be substituted with gluten-free flour for coeliacs), adding herbs and – sometimes – spices before binding the dough ingredients together with water.

A good way to check if the food within the salt-dough shell is cooked is to use a metal skewer and insert it into the centre. Using this method to test for doneness means you can tell how soft vegetables are, and also how warm the centre of meat joints are, by holding the end of the skewer that has just been inserted on the inside of your wrist to gauge the temperature.

Once the item is baked, do not leave the salt dough on for too long as the salt will continue to permeate through it and it can become over-seasoned.

SALT DOUGH

Mix the ingredients together and bind with 100ml cold water to form a dough. Roll out the dough on a sheet of baking parchment to a thickness of 2mm, then wrap it around the vegetable or joint of meat until it is completely enclosed. Place the dough-wrapped ingredient on the lined baking sheet and bake for the time given in the recipe.

100g rock salt
200g plain flour
chopped herbs of choice

INGREDIENT	SALT-DOUGH QUANTITY	HERBS/SPICES
Root vegetables	1 quantity	Lavender, nutmeg, thyme, rosemary, bay leaves
Whole fish	1 quantity	Dill, thyme, rosemary, bay leaves, lavender, basil, lemongrass
Whole poultry	2 quantities	Tarragon, thyme, rosemary, oregano, bay leaves
Joints of meat	2 quantities	Lavender, thyme, rosemary, bay leaves

Salt-baking is a whole new way to enhance the parsnip's sweetness and add to its savouriness. Parsnip and horseradish are, for me, a natural food match like tomato and basil. I really like the heat the horseradish adds to this dish, while also adding a little acidity to break through the creaminess. This is a winter dish that is great for a cold evening to warm and satisfy.

SALT-BAKED PARSNIP AND HORSERADISH CRUMBLE

Preheat the oven to 200°C/180°C fan/gas 6.

To make the salt dough, combine all ingredients in a bowl with 100–125ml cold water (enough to bind the mixture). Knead until well combined. Roll out the dough on a sheet of baking parchment to a thickness of 2mm, then place the parsnips, top to tail, on top. Fold the dough on top of the parsnips until the parsnips are completely enclosed and place the dough-wrapped parsnips on a baking sheet. Bake for 1 hour until the parsnips are soft (breaking the crust a little to test for doneness with a knife).

While the parsnips are baking, make the horseradish sauce. Put the milk and thyme in a saucepan and bring to a simmer. Remove from the heat and cover with clingfilm. Set aside for 20 minutes then strain through a fine sieve into a jug. Add the cream and horseradish and season well with sea salt and pepper.

Remove the parsnips from the oven and, using a knife, carefully remove the salt dough and discard. Leave the parsnips to cool, then cut them into 2–3cm-thick rounds. Put them in the bottom of a large, ovenproof dish (approximately 20cm square). Pour the horseradish sauce over the top of the parsnips.

To make the crumble, mix all ingredients together in a bowl. Season well then crumble on top of the parsnips and horseradish sauce.

Bake for 20–25 minutes until golden, then sprinkle over the remaining thyme.

Serves: 4
Preparation time: 30 minutes
Cooking time: 1 hour 25 minutes

6–8 parsnips, peeled and topped and tailed (about 1kg in total)

FOR THE SALT DOUGH
1 x quantity of Salt Dough (page 31), using 1 tbsp roughly chopped thyme

FOR THE HORSERADISH SAUCE
400ml milk
½ bunch of thyme
150ml double cream
3 tbsp horseradish sauce
sea salt and freshly ground black pepper

FOR THE CRUMBLE TOPPING
150g wholemeal flour
50g rolled oats
100g soft butter
50g grated Cheddar cheese
2 tbsp thyme leaves, plus extra to serve

Kabocha squash is a small and sweet, dry-fleshed pumpkin. Salt-baking really brings alive the flavour of the squash and enhances its sweetness. The combination of the sweet pumpkin flesh with the creamy ricotta and tangy pomegranate makes a great meal. Add the freshness of the mint and the crunch of the toasted seeds and it's a winner.

SALT-BAKED KABOCHA SQUASH, POMEGRANATE, RICOTTA AND MINT

Preheat the oven to 200°C/180°C fan/gas 6 and line a baking sheet and baking tray with baking parchment.

To make the salt dough, combine all the ingredients in a bowl with 125–150ml cold water (enough to bind the mixture). Knead until well combined. Roll out the dough on a sheet of baking parchment to a thickness of 2mm then wrap it around the squash until it is completely enclosed. Place the dough-wrapped squash on the lined baking sheet and bake for 1½ hours until soft (breaking the crust a little to test for doneness with a knife).

While the squash is cooking, coat the pumpkin seeds with the soy sauce and vegetable oil in a bowl. Tip onto the lined baking tray, spread them out and bake for 8 minutes. Remove and allow to cool.

Whisk the ricotta and lemon zest in a bowl and season to taste with sea salt and pepper.

Whisk the pomegranate molasses with the olive oil in a separate bowl.

Remove the squash from the oven and, using a knife, carefully remove the salt dough from the squash and discard. Leave the squash to cool, then scoop the flesh from the skin, leaving it in large chunks.

To assemble, place the chunks of squash on a large platter or divide between four plates. Dollop the ricotta on top and drizzle with the pomegranate dressing. Garnish with the pumpkin and pomegranate seeds. Scatter over the mint and serve.

Serves: 4
Preparation time: 25 minutes
Cooking time: 1 hour 30 minutes, plus cooling

1 kabocha or other small squash
60g pumpkin seeds
½ tbsp soy sauce
½ tbsp vegetable oil
200g ricotta cheese
grated zest of 1 lemon
4 tbsp pomegranate molasses
50ml olive oil
seeds from 1 small pomegranate
sea salt and freshly ground black pepper
½ bunch of mint, to serve

FOR THE SALT DOUGH
1 x quantity of Salt Dough (page 31), using 1½ tbsp chopped rosemary

Tempura is always a treat but generally it is reserved for fish or seafood. This recipe uses fennel, which has a lovely flavour when it's effectively 'steamed' in the light, crisp batter. In this recipe, there are also two other unusual elements – a fennel 'marmalade' whereby the fennel is caramelised and releases its own sugars to create a sweet condiment, and a vegan aioli made with chickpea water.

TEMPURA FENNEL WITH FENNEL MARMALADE AND GARLIC AIOLI

Serves: 4 as a starter
Preparation time: 25 minutes
Cooking time: around 1 hour

2 tbsp vegetable oil, plus extra for
    deep-frying
1 fennel bulb, finely sliced, plus
    1 bunch baby fennel bulbs, each
    bulb halved lengthways
grated zest and juice of 1 lemon
sea salt and freshly ground black
    pepper

FOR THE AIOLI
60g aquafaba (the liquid from a 400g
    tin of chickpeas, strained through
    a sieve)
1 tbsp white wine vinegar
1 garlic clove, finely grated
½ tsp Dijon mustard
175ml olive oil
50ml vegetable oil
½ tsp table salt

FOR THE TEMPURA BATTER
6 tbsp cornflour
3 tbsp plain flour, plus extra for
    dusting
3–6 tbsp soda water

Heat the 2 tablespoons of vegetable oil in a medium saucepan over medium heat. When hot, add the finely sliced fennel. Season lightly with sea salt, reduce the heat and cook gently for 40–50 minutes, stirring regularly, until it caramelises and turns a dark golden brown. Add half the lemon zest and juice and cook for a further 2 minutes. Remove from the heat, transfer to a dish and leave to cool.

To make the aioli, put the aquafaba in a bowl and, using a balloon whisk, mix in the vinegar, garlic and Dijon mustard. Put both oils in a jug and slowly drizzle them into the aquafaba mixture, whisking continuously as you do so. When it reaches a thick mayonnaise consistency, season with table salt and the remaining lemon zest and juice.

To make the tempura batter, mix the flours together in a bowl with a pinch of sea salt and a pinch of pepper. Gradually whisk in enough of the soda water to make a thick batter.

Pour enough vegetable oil into a deep-fat fryer or large, deep saucepan to come up to 6cm and heat to 180°C.

Dust the baby fennel slices in the flour then, one by one, dip them in the tempura batter and carefully place them in the hot oil. Fry (in batches) for 4–6 minutes until golden and crisp. Remove with a slotted spoon and transfer to kitchen paper to remove any excess oil.

Serve the tempura immediately, with the marmalade and aioli.

There are many versions of classic pasta dishes but this take on squash pasta is such a great comfort food. This is a relatively quick but very tasty dish which satisfies the whole family at my house. The savouriness of the sage adds an extra lift. You can use dried or fresh pasta.

TAGLIATELLE WITH BUTTERNUT SQUASH, HAZELNUTS AND CRISPY SAGE

Put the diced squash in a medium saucepan, cover with cold water, season with a generous pinch of salt and add the bay leaves and thyme. Bring to the boil and simmer for 20–25 minutes until tender, then strain off the water and remove the bay leaves and thyme sprigs.

Add the nutmeg and 25g of the butter and lightly mash the squash. Season to taste and keep warm.

Heat the remaining 50g butter in a large frying pan over high heat. When foaming, add the hazelnuts and sage. Season with sea salt and pepper and cook for 5–8 minutes until golden and crispy, and the butter has browned.

Cook the tagliatelle according to the packet instructions. Drain and mix with most of the hazelnut and sage butter. Gently mix through the butternut squash mash and serve, topped with the remaining hazelnut, sage and brown butter.

Serves: 4
Preparation time: 15 minutes
Cooking time: 35 minutes

1 butternut squash, peeled, halved, deseeded and diced
2 bay leaves
4 sprigs of thyme
½ nutmeg, grated
75g butter
80g blanched hazelnuts, roughly chopped
20 sage leaves
350g tagliatelle pasta
sea salt and freshly ground black pepper

These fritters make a lovely summery meal – fresh, vibrant and full of nutrients. They are simple to make and if you choose a vegan cheese they can be vegan friendly, too. Try to use whole spices rather than ground, toasting them and crushing them when required; the flavour is much more intense. The cashew salad adds a lovely richness to the dish.

COURGETTE, SPELT AND CUMIN FRITTERS

Put the grated courgette in a colander, sprinkle with the 2 teaspoons of table salt and toss to distribute the salt. Set the colander over a bowl or the sink and leave for 30 minutes to drain.

Cook the spelt according to the packet instructions. Drain well. Heat 2 tablespoons of the vegetable oil in a frying pan over medium heat. When hot, add the shallots and garlic and cook for 5–7 minutes until soft but not browned. Add the cumin, mix well, then transfer to a bowl.

Put the grated courgettes in a clean tea towel and squeeze out as much of the liquid as possible. Tip them into the bowl with the shallots and garlic. Add the flour and lemon zest and mix well. Add 2 tablespoons of the chopped parsley, the cheese, cooked spelt, mustard powder and a generous twist of black pepper. Fry a little of the mix in a pan with a little oil, taste to check the seasoning and add more salt if necessary. Shape the mixture into 12 balls, then flatten into patties.

To make the vinaigrette, whisk the olive oil, white wine vinegar and wholegrain mustard together in a bowl. Set aside. Slice the remaining green courgette into circles then mix with the yellow ribbons, the remaining chopped parsley and the cashew nuts.

Heat the remaining 2 tablespoons of vegetable oil in a large, non-stick frying pan over medium heat. When hot, add half the patties and fry for about 5 minutes on each side, until golden on the outside and cooked through. Repeat with the remaining patties.

To serve, place two fritters on each plate, dress the courgette ribbons and rounds with the vinaigrette, season with sea salt and pepper and serve alongside the fritters.

Serves: 4
Preparation time: 25 minutes, plus 30 minutes salting
Cooking time: about 50 minutes

5 green courgettes, 4 coarsely grated (around 1kg total grated weight)
2 tsp table salt
1 yellow courgette, sliced into ribbons
80g cashew nuts, roasted and roughly chopped

FOR THE FRITTERS
100g spelt
4 tbsp vegetable oil, plus extra for frying
4 shallots, finely diced
1 garlic clove, finely grated
2 tbsp cumin seeds, toasted and crushed
4 tbsp plain flour, plus extra for coating
grated zest of ½ lemon
3 tbsp finely chopped flat-leaf parsley
70g grated vegan cheese or Cheddar cheese
½ tsp English mustard powder
sea salt and freshly ground black pepper

FOR THE VINAIGRETTE
4 tbsp olive oil
1 tbsp white wine vinegar
½ tsp wholegrain mustard

These 'ravioli' are made with dumpling wrappers rather than pasta. They are very handy to have in the freezer for when you want to make this modern version of ravioli. It's the perfect way to practise your ravioli-making skills without having to make fresh pasta. This whole dish is also dairy-free and egg-free.

MUSHROOM 'RAVIOLI' WITH SHALLOT SAUCE AND GRILLED SPRING ONIONS

To make the mushroom filling, heat the vegetable oil in a large saucepan over medium heat. Add the diced shallot and cook for 7–10 minutes, until soft but not brown. Increase the heat to medium-high, add the mushrooms, thyme, bay leaf and season well with sea salt. Cook for about 10 minutes until all of the liquid from the mushrooms has evaporated, then add the Madeira and cook until it has evaporated. Remove the thyme sprigs and bay leaf and place the mushroom mix in a container. Cover and chill.

To make the shallot sauce, heat the vegetable oil in a medium saucepan over medium-high heat. Add the sliced shallots, season with sea salt, and cook for 5–7 minutes, stirring regularly, until they are a deep golden colour. Add the balsamic vinegar and simmer until all the liquid has evaporated. Add the coconut milk and simmer for 5 minutes. Place in a blender and blitz until smooth, then pass through a fine sieve into a bowl to remove any lumps.

To make the ravioli, gently brush the outside edges of one of the gyoza wrappers with a little water. Place a scant tablespoon of the mushroom filling in the centre and place another gyoza wrapper on top. Press the edges to seal, making sure you remove any air trapped inside. Continue with the remaining wrappers and filling until you have 12 ravioli. Arrange them in a single layer in a steamer set over a pan of boiling water (you may need to steam them in batches, keeping the cooked dumplings hot while you cook the rest). Steam for 5–7 minutes.

For the spring onions, heat a griddle pan until smoking. Drizzle the trimmed onions with the olive oil, season and grill until just blackened.

Serve 3 ravioli per portion, with the shallot sauce and grilled spring onions.

Serves: 4 (makes 12 'ravioli')
Preparation time: 35 minutes,
    plus cooling
Cooking time: around 1 hour
    10 minutes

24 gyoza wrappers
1 bunch of spring onions, roots
    trimmed off
1 tbsp olive oil
sea salt

FOR THE MUSHROOM FILLING
1 tbsp vegetable oil
1 shallot, finely diced
2 flat-cap mushrooms, finely diced
    (around 175g)
2 sprigs of thyme
1 bay leaf
15ml Madeira wine

FOR THE SHALLOT SAUCE
2 tbsp vegetable oil
4 shallots, finely sliced
4 tbsp balsamic vinegar
400ml coconut milk

This is the perfect dish for an impressive but light summer lunch, when tomatoes are at their finest and the rosé is flowing. Filo pastry is a versatile product to always have in the fridge, given it can be used for sweet and savoury dishes and is rather quick to cook. It's dairy-free and egg-free, too.

HERITAGE TOMATO, SESAME AND MISO TARTS

Preheat the oven to 200°C/180°C fan/gas 6.

Brush each layer of the filo with olive oil and layer one on top of the other. Brush the top with more oil (you'll use about 5 tablespoons oil in total) and sprinkle it with the sesame seeds. Trim the edges then cut the layered filo stack into eight 8 x 12cm rectangles. Place them between two sheets of baking parchment then put on a baking sheet, with another baking sheet on top to keep the filo flat. Bake for 6–8 minutes, then remove the top baking sheet and the top sheet of baking parchment and bake for a further 8–10 minutes, until golden. Remove from the oven and leave to cool on a wire rack to crisp up.

To make the tomato sauce, blitz the semi-dried tomatoes in a blender or food processor with the tomato purée, olive oil and parsley. Taste and adjust seasoning if necessary.

To make the tahini-miso dressing, whisk the tahini, rice wine vinegar, miso paste and olive oil together in a bowl. Add a few tablespoons of water if it is too thick – it needs to be drizzling consistency.

Slice the tomatoes and drizzle them with the remaining 2 tablespoons of olive oil. Season with sea salt and pepper.

To assemble the tarts, divide the semi-dried tomato mix evenly between the eight filo rectangles, spreading out evenly over the pastry. Top with the sliced tomatoes then drizzle with the tahini-miso dressing. Place one rectangle on top of another and garnish with black sesame seeds and parsley.

Makes: 4 tarts
Preparation time: 25 minutes
Cooking time: 20 minutes, plus
    cooling

6 sheets filo pastry
7 tbsp olive oil
1 tbsp black sesame seeds, plus extra
    to serve
4–8 Heritage tomatoes (depending on
    their size)
flat-leaf parsley, to serve
sea salt and freshly ground black
    pepper

FOR THE TOMATO SAUCE
75g semi-dried tomatoes
1 tsp tomato purée
4 tsp olive oil
1 tbsp chopped flat-leaf parsley

FOR THE TAHINI-MISO DRESSING
2 tbsp tahini
2 tbsp rice wine vinegar
1 tbsp white miso paste
2 tbsp olive oil

Baked cannelloni is a great dish to make in advance, as it gets better when left in the fridge for a day or two. So it's perfect for a make-ahead family meal on a weeknight, or a treat at the weekend. The trick to making cannelloni is to ensure there is enough liquid during cooking for the dried pasta to absorb, as well as to coat the pasta tubes for serving. Cottage cheese works as a great substitute for ricotta, too, and can add a little more texture to the overall dish.

SPINACH, RICOTTA AND BASIL PESTO CANNELLONI

Preheat the oven to 200°C/180°C fan/gas 6.

To make the tomato sauce, heat the oil in a saucepan over medium heat and add the onion and garlic. Cook for 10 minutes until soft and golden, stirring frequently. Add the remaining sauce ingredients, season with sea salt and pepper and bring to a simmer. Cook over medium heat for 30 minutes, stirring occasionally. Transfer to a blender or use a stick blender to blitz the sauce to a smooth consistency, then leave to cool.

While the tomato sauce is cooking, make the white sauce. Put the milk in a small saucepan, stud the onion with the cloves and add it to the milk along with the bay leaf. Gently bring to the boil over low heat. Remove from the heat and leave to infuse for a few minutes before removing the bay leaf and onion.

Melt the butter in a saucepan over low heat and add the flour and a pinch each of sea salt and pepper. Cook for about 1 minute to get rid of the floury taste, but avoid letting it brown. Add a ladle of the warm milk and stir to combine. Continue adding the milk, a little at a time, until it's all incorporated. Bring to the boil then simmer gently for a few minutes, until you have a thick pouring sauce. Keep warm, over very low heat or off the heat covered with a lid, while you prepare the rest of the ingredients for the cannelloni.

Serves: 4–6
Preparation time: around 1 hour
Cooking time: 1 hour 30 minutes

500g baby spinach leaves
500g ricotta cheese, drained
200g grated Cheddar cheese
½ nutmeg, finely grated
250g dried cannelloni tubes
100g grated Gruyère cheese
sea salt and freshly ground black pepper

FOR THE TOMATO SAUCE
1 tbsp vegetable oil
1 onion, sliced
1 garlic clove, crushed
400g tomato passata or 1 × 400g tin chopped tomatoes
1 tbsp tomato purée
2 tbsp balsamic vinegar
2 tbsp Worcestershire sauce
50ml Vegetable Stock (page 57)

Bring a large pan of salted water to the boil and blanch the spinach for 1 minute. Refresh under cold running water and drain well. Squeeze out the excess moisture from the leaves and roughly chop.

Mix the ricotta with the Cheddar cheese and grated nutmeg in a bowl and season to taste with sea salt and pepper. Add the spinach and mix well.

To make the basil pesto, put the pine nuts on a baking tray and toast them in the oven for 6 minutes, shaking the tray halfway through. Remove from the oven and leave to cool, and reduce the oven temperature to 190°C/170°C fan/gas 5. Put the basil, Parmesan, garlic, oil and toasted pine nuts in a blender and blitz to form a chunky pesto. Season well.

Put the ricotta and spinach mix in a piping bag and pipe it into the cannelloni tubes. Lay the filled cannelloni tubes in one layer in a large lasagne dish and cover with a layer of tomato sauce and basil pesto. Cover the cannelloni with the cheese sauce, scatter over the grated Gruyère and season with sea salt and pepper.

Bake for 45–50 minutes until the sauce is bubbling and the pasta is al dente.

FOR THE WHITE SAUCE
600ml milk
1 small onion, peeled but left whole
10 cloves
1 bay leaf
50g butter
50g plain flour

FOR THE BASIL PESTO
40g pine nuts
1 bunch of basil, leaves only
30g grated Parmesan cheese
2 garlic cloves, crushed
100ml olive oil

Kabocha squash are the ideal variety of squash for this recipe as they have a low moisture content so the pastry will remain deliciously crisp. The pairing with Parmesan and rosemary complements the sweetness of the squash perfectly. I love to make this at the end of summer and serve it with a green salad for a tasty weekend lunch.

KABOCHA SQUASH, PARMESAN AND ROSEMARY TART

Preheat the oven to 210°C/190°C fan/gas 7 and line a baking tray with baking parchment.

Slice each squash half into 1cm-thick slices and place them in a single layer on a roasting tray. Drizzle with the oil and season liberally with salt and pepper. Bake for 15–20 minutes until just tender.

Lay the pastry out flat on the lined baking tray and carefully score a 1cm border around the edge.

Place the rosemary, pine nuts, half the Parmesan, the garlic, olive oil and a pinch of sea salt in a tall container and blend using a stick blender. Add the mascarpone and pulse until combined.

Spread the mix inside the border on the puff pastry. Lay the squash slices over the mix and finish with a good dose of black pepper.

Bake for 30–35 minutes until golden. Sprinkle over the remaining Parmesan and place back in the oven until the cheese melts. Serve hot.

Serves: 6
Preparation time: 20 minutes
Cooking time: about 1 hour

1 kabocha or butternut squash,
    peeled, halved and deseeded
2 tbsp vegetable oil
1 x 320g sheet of ready-rolled
    all-butter puff pastry
1 tbsp finely chopped rosemary
30g pine nuts
60g grated Parmesan cheese
1 garlic clove, finely grated
50ml olive oil
3 tbsp mascarpone
sea salt and freshly ground black
    pepper

Tofu itself is a rather flavourless ingredient, however it does add a good texture to dishes. If you have never been a fan then do try this dish as the flavours work really well together and create a tasty and wholesome meal. Always use firm tofu, and preferably a refrigerated product, not an ambient, shelf-stocked one, as the flavour and texture are much better.

BRAISED TOFU WITH BUCKWHEAT, CAVALO NERO AND CAPERS

Heat the vegetable oil in a deep frying pan over high heat. When hot, add the onions, season with sea salt and pepper and cook for 15–20 minutes until golden and caramelised.

Meanwhile, toast the buckwheat in a dry frying pan for 5 minutes over medium heat, then cook it according to the packet instructions. Drain well and stir through the olive oil. Keep warm.

Add the garlic and chilli to the onions and cook for a further 4 minutes, until soft, then add the balsamic vinegar and cook until it coats the onion mix. Add the thyme, tomato purée, Worcestershire sauce and 200ml of the vegetable stock and mix well. Simmer rapidly for 5 minutes.

Scatter the tofu in the frying pan on top of the onion mixture. Reduce the heat to low and cook the tofu for 10 minutes.

Add the cavolo nero to the pan with the capers. Add the remaining vegetable stock. Cover the frying pan and cook gently for about 5 minutes, or until the cavolo nero is cooked. Stir to combine.

Spoon the buckwheat into bowls then top it with the braised tofu, cavolo nero and caper sauce.

Serves: 4
Preparation time: 15 minutes
Cooking time: about 50 minutes

2 tbsp vegetable oil
2 onions, thinly sliced
200g buckwheat
2 tbsp olive oil
2 garlic cloves, finely grated
½ red chilli, deseeded and finely diced
2 tbsp balsamic vinegar
1 tbsp picked thyme leaves
2 tbsp tomato purée
2 tbsp Worcestershire sauce
300ml Vegetable Stock (page 57)
350g firm tofu, cut into 5mm dice
200g cavolo nero or kale, tough stems removed and leaves roughly sliced
3 tbsp capers in brine, strained and finely chopped
sea salt and freshly ground black pepper

A bhaji is an Indian fritter, typically made with onions and loads of spices. I have used cauliflower along with the onion, as it gives the bhajis a slight nuttiness. The sweet, slightly spiced yoghurt is a great accompaniment, too.

CAULIFLOWER BHAJIS WITH MANGO AND CORIANDER YOGHURT

Melt the butter in a medium frying pan over medium-high heat. When hot, add the onions, season with sea salt and cook for about 5 minutes, then reduce the heat to medium and cook for a further 30 minutes, stirring frequently, until the onions are golden and caramelised. Add the grated cauliflower and cook for a further 4 minutes.

To make the spice mix, toast the ingredients in a small dry frying pan over medium heat until fragrant and the mustard seeds begin to pop. Remove from the heat and grind to a powder in a spice grinder or pestle and mortar.

Place the onion and cauliflower mix into a large bowl. Add the spice mix and mix well. Mix in the chilli, coriander and egg. Add the chickpea flour and baking powder and fold gently to just combine. Season with a pinch of salt and pepper.

To make the mango and coriander yoghurt, whisk all of the ingredients together in a bowl and season to taste.

Pour enough vegetable oil into a deep-fat fryer or large, deep saucepan to come up to 6cm and heat it to 160°C. Carefully place spoonfuls of the bhaji mix in the hot oil and fry in batches for 3–4 minutes until deep golden and crisp. Remove with a slotted spoon and transfer to kitchen paper, to soak up any excess oil. Season with sea salt and serve with the yoghurt.

Serves: 4 as a starter (makes about 16 bhajis)
Preparation time: 25 minutes
Cooking time: around 50 minutes

25g butter
2 onions, finely sliced
1 cauliflower, grated (a box grater works well)
1 green chilli, deseeded and finely diced
3 tbsp chopped coriander
1 egg
125g chickpea flour
½ tsp baking powder
vegetable oil, for deep-frying
sea salt and freshly ground black pepper

FOR THE SPICE MIX
1 tsp ground turmeric
1 tsp cumin seeds
¼ tsp coriander seeds
¼ tsp black mustard seeds
½ tsp garam masala

FOR THE MANGO AND CORIANDER YOGHURT
2 tbsp mango chutney
1 tbsp finely chopped coriander
½ tsp nigella seeds
1 tsp sriracha sauce (hot chilli sauce)
100g Greek yoghurt

This is my take on classic Friday night comfort food. Making your own curry paste really enhances the flavour of any curry, so I really recommend giving it a go. Using two chillies does create a spicy sauce, so if you prefer less heat then stick to just the one. You can find coriander with its roots intact at Indian grocers or specialist grocers, though if you can't find it, regular coriander (just the leaves and stems) will do just fine.

THAI VEGETABLE CURRY

To make the curry paste, put all the ingredients in a blender or food processor and blitz until smooth.

Heat the vegetable oil in a large saucepan over medium heat. When hot, add the curry paste and fry for 4–5 minutes, stirring, until very fragrant.

Add the fish sauce and palm sugar and cook for 3 minutes. Add the coconut milk and vegetable stock and simmer gently for 20 minutes. Strain the sauce through a fine sieve into a clean saucepan, discarding the remnants in the sieve.

Bring the curry sauce to a simmer and season to taste with salt (if needed). Add the sweet potato and cook for 10 minutes, then add the mushrooms and cook for a further 10 minutes.

Cook the broccoli in a separate pan of boiling water for 6 minutes, until tender.

Add the broccoli, peas and water chestnuts to the curry, heat through and serve with fluffy rice.

Serves: 4
Preparation time: 20 minutes
Cooking time: around 50 minutes

2 tbsp vegetable oil
4 tbsp fish sauce
15g palm sugar
400ml coconut milk
400ml Vegetable Stock (page 57)
2 sweet potatoes (around 600g), peeled and diced into approx. 1.5cm cubes
12 button mushrooms, quartered
8 stalks Tenderstem broccoli
100g fresh or frozen peas
1 x 220g tin sliced water chestnuts, drained

FOR THE GREEN CURRY PASTE
2 green chillies, deseeded and roughly chopped
3 shallots, peeled
4cm piece of fresh ginger, peeled and roughly chopped
2 lemongrass stalks
1 bunch of coriander (stalks and roots if possible)
2 garlic cloves, peeled
½ tsp table salt
grated zest and juice of 1 lime

Freekeh is a roasted green wheat that that brings out nuttiness and earthiness in this tagine. It is similar in texture to bulgur wheat but is a little softer. It is readily available in most supermarkets. This is a great midweek meal as it is quick to prepare, but also very satisfying.

AUBERGINE, FREEKEH AND CASHEW TAGINE

Serves: 4
Preparation time: 30 minutes
Cooking time: 1 hour 30 minutes

100g cashew nuts
200g freekeh
6 tbsp vegetable oil
2 large onions, finely chopped
3 garlic cloves, crushed
2cm piece of fresh ginger, peeled and grated
2 tbsp tomato purée
400ml tomato passata or 1 x 400g tin chopped tomatoes
250ml Vegetable Stock (page 57)
1 tbsp sherry vinegar
1 tsp black treacle
50g dried currants
2 tsp saffron stands, soaked in 1 tbsp warm water for 10 minutes
2 aubergines, cut into 2cm dice
1 bunch of coriander, leaves chopped
sea salt and freshly ground black pepper

Preheat the oven to 200°C/180°C fan/gas 6.

Put the cashew nuts on a roasting tray and bake for 6–10 minutes until golden. Remove, leave to cool, then chop roughly. Reduce the oven temperature to 160°C/140°C fan/gas 3.

Cook the freekeh for half of the time on the packet instructions, then drain.

Heat 2 tablespoons of the vegetable oil in a large casserole dish over medium heat. Add the onions, season with sea salt and pepper and sauté for about 10 minutes until they are soft but not coloured. Add the garlic and ginger for the last 3–4 minutes. Add the tomato purée, the passata or chopped tomatoes, stock, vinegar, treacle, currants and saffron to the casserole and remove from the heat.

Heat a dry large frying pan over high heat and, when hot, add the spices from the spice mix ingredients and stir them for 3–4 minutes until fragrant. Transfer the spices to a mortar and crush with the pestle. Mix with the flour and table salt in a bowl.

Add 2 tablespoons of vegetable oil to the frying pan and place back on the heat. Season the diced aubergine generously with the spiced flour and fry it in the oil, in batches, until golden, adding more oil with each batch as necessary.

Add half of the chopped coriander to the casserole and mix well. Add the part-cooked freekeh and the spiced aubergine. Sprinkle with three-quarters of the cashew nuts.

Bring to the boil, cover with a lid and transfer to the oven for around 1 hour until the freekeh is tender and the sauce thickened. Serve sprinkled with the remaining coriander and cashew nuts.

FOR THE SPICE MIX
2 tbsp cumin seeds
1 tbsp fennel seeds
1 tbsp yellow mustard seeds
1 tsp coriander seeds
1 tsp ground turmeric
1 tsp ground cinnamon
1 tsp sweet smoked paprika
2 tbsp plain flour
½ tsp table salt

A well-made risotto is something that takes time and cannot be rushed, but the end result is well worth it. Ensure you use a decent stock – it will really enhance the flavour and texture of the finished dish. This is the perfect opportunity to make your own stock, which will add a whole other dimension to your risotto. Always use carnaroli or Vialone Nano rice: the short, plump grains cook slowly with the centre remaining al dente.

CARAMELISED CELERIAC, THYME AND HAZELNUT RISOTTO

Preheat the oven to 180°C/160°C fan/gas 4.

Place the hazelnuts on a baking tray and drizzle with 1 tablespoon of the vegetable oil. Season well with sea salt and pepper and bake for 6–8 minutes until golden. Remove from the oven and allow to cool, then finely chop and set aside.

Melt the butter in a large saucepan over medium-high heat. When hot, add the celeriac and season with sea salt. Cook for 10–15 minutes, stirring, until the celeriac is soft and deep golden brown. Remove half of the celeriac and set aside. Add the milk to the saucepan and bring to a simmer for a few minutes. Scrape the bottom of the pan well then transfer everything to a blender or food processor and blend until smooth. Wipe out the pan.

Put the stock in a separate saucepan with the string-tied thyme sprigs and bring to the boil. Reduce the heat and simmer gently. Note: the thyme sprigs are to flavour the stock, not to use in the risotto, so discard them when you are getting down to the last few ladlefuls.

Heat the remaining 2 tablespoons of vegetable oil over medium heat in the saucepan you cooked the celeriac in. Add the shallots and garlic and cook for a few minutes until the shallots have softened but not coloured. Add the rice and stir for a few minutes until it becomes shiny and translucent. When it starts to make a faint popping sound, add the wine and let it bubble away and reduce, stirring continuously. Add a ladleful of the hot stock and some sea salt and pepper and stir. Simmer and continue stirring until the stock has been absorbed by the rice. Cook the rice for 15–20 minutes, adding the remaining stock a ladleful at a time, stirring continuously until each

Serves: 4–6
Preparation time: 15 minutes
Cooking time: around 40 minutes

60g blanched hazelnuts
3 tbsp vegetable oil
50g butter
1 celeriac (around 500g), peeled and cut into 1cm dice
100ml milk
approx. 1.3 litres Chicken or Vegetable Stock (pages 83 and 57)
½ bunch of thyme, with 1 tbsp picked leaves, the remainder tied together with string
2 shallots, finely chopped
1 garlic clove, finely grated
500g carnaroli or Vialone Nano risotto rice
125ml dry white wine
75g grated Parmesan cheese
sea salt and freshly ground black pepper
extra virgin olive oil, or hazelnut oil, to serve

ladleful has been absorbed before adding the next. The risotto is cooked when the rice grains are a little firm but don't have any chalky crunch on the outside when bitten into.

Stir in the caramelised celeriac purée and allow the risotto to come to a simmer. Stir in most of the Parmesan, adding any extra stock if required. Finally, add the diced caramelised celeriac and most of the thyme leaves.

Taste, add a little more salt and pepper if you like and serve straight away, sprinkled with the chopped hazelnuts, the remaining Parmesan, a drizzle of extra virgin olive oil or hazelnut oil and the remaining thyme leaves.

VEGETABLE STOCK

Put the leeks, carrots, onions, celery and garlic in a large stock pot and cover with 2 litres of cold water. Bring to the boil over high heat. Skim off any scum, reduce the heat to medium and cook for 8 minutes.

Lightly crush the star anise, coriander seeds and white peppercorns in a pestle and mortar or on a hard surface with the bottom of a heavy pan. As soon as the 8 minutes are up, add the crushed spices to the stock pot along with the fresh herbs. Simmer for a further 2 minutes, then remove from the heat. Leave to cool, then cover and transfer to the fridge for 24 hours.

Strain the vegetable stock through a fine sieve and discard the vegetables. Keep covered in the fridge and use within 3–4 days. Alternatively, freeze and use within 4 months.

Makes: approx. 1.5 litres
Preparation time: 20 minutes,
    plus 24 hours chilling
Cooking time: 10 minutes

2 leeks, chopped
6 carrots, chopped
3 onions, chopped
3 celery sticks, chopped
4 garlic cloves
1 star anise
1 tsp coriander seeds
½ tsp white peppercorns
2 bay leaves
¼ bunch of thyme

This is such a classic Italian dish. I have lovely memories of eating a great version of this in Italy, at a small, family-run trattoria. The seasoning, texture and flavour were perfect, so this is my attempt at recreating it, outside of Italy!

AUBERGINE PARMIGIANA

Serves: 4–6
Preparation time: 30 minutes, plus
   1 hour of salting of aubergines
Cooking time: around 2 hours

Sprinkle the aubergine slices, on both sides, with table salt and pack them in a colander. Set the colander over a bowl for 1 hour while the moisture is extracted from the aubergine.

Meanwhile, make the tomato sauce. Heat the butter in a large saucepan over medium heat and add the onion and garlic. Cook for 10 minutes until golden, then add the red wine and cook until it has reduced to a syrup. Add the remaining sauce ingredients, season with sea salt and pepper, bring to a simmer and cook for 30 minutes, stirring occasionally. Transfer to a blender or use a stick blender to blitz the sauce to a smooth consistency.

Preheat the oven to 200°C/180°C fan/gas 6, rinse the aubergine slices under cold running water and pat them dry with kitchen paper.

Pour enough vegetable oil into a large, deep frying pan to come up to approximately 1cm and place over high heat. When hot, dust the aubergine slices with flour then fry them, in batches, until golden, crispy on the outside and slightly soft. Add more oil to the pan as needed. Remove and transfer to sheets of kitchen paper to soak up the excess oil.

Place a layer of half the fried aubergine slices on the base of a deep, large ovenproof dish (approximately 20 x 30cm). Top with a layer of half the tomato sauce, then add a layer of half the mozzarella slices and sprinkle over some of the Parmesan. Repeat the layering again to use up all the aubergine, tomato sauce and cheese.

To make the crumb, mix the breadcrumbs with the soft butter then add the other ingredients. Mix well then season with sea salt and pepper. Cover the aubergines in the breadcrumb mix and bake the Parmigiana in the oven for 40–50 minutes until the top is golden brown.

4 aubergines, cut widthways into
   1cm-thick slices
table salt
vegetable oil, for shallow-frying
plain flour, for dusting
3 x 125g balls mozzarella, sliced as
   thinly as possible
100g grated Parmesan cheese

FOR THE TOMATO SAUCE
50g butter
2 onions, thinly sliced
4 garlic cloves, finely grated
200ml red wine
800g tomato passata or 2 x 400g tins
   chopped tomatoes
2 tbsp tomato purée
2 tbsp balsamic vinegar
2 tbsp Worcestershire sauce
½ bunch of sage, leaves finely
   chopped
sea salt and freshly ground black
   pepper

FOR THE CRUMB
40g panko breadcrumbs
1 tbsp soft butter
50g grated Parmesan cheese
½ bunch of basil, leaves finely sliced
20g pine nuts, toasted and finely
   chopped

Vegetable lasagne is a great way to get kids to enjoy eating greens. Change the vegetables you use according to what you have in the fridge, or if you have anything that needs using up. We love lasagne at the weekends in our house. This is great for vegetarians but you won't find your meat-eating friends complaining as it's completely delicious.

SUMMER VEGETABLE LASAGNE

To make the tomato sauce, heat 2 tablespoons of the vegetable oil in a saucepan. Add the onion, garlic and a generous pinch each of sea salt and pepper and cook over medium-low heat for 10 minutes until golden. Add the remaining sauce ingredients, bring to a simmer and cook for 30 minutes, stirring occasionally. Transfer to a blender or use a stick blender to blitz the sauce to a smooth consistency. Season to taste and leave to cool.

To make the white sauce, put the milk in a small saucepan. Stud the onion with the cloves and add it to the milk along with the bay leaf. Gently bring to the boil over low heat. Remove from the heat and leave to infuse for a few minutes before removing the bay leaf and onion.

Melt the butter in a saucepan and add the flour, and a good pinch of sea salt and pepper. Cook over low heat for about 1 minute, stirring, to get rid of the floury taste, but avoid letting it brown. Add a ladleful of the infused milk and whisk to combine. Continue adding the milk, a little at a time, bring to the boil, then simmer gently for a few minutes, until you have a thick pouring sauce. Keep warm over low heat.

Heat a griddle pan over high heat and, when it's smoking, drizzle the courgette slices with the remaining 2 tablespoons of vegetable oil, season with sea salt, and chargrill on each side until cooked, for a total of 7 minutes.

Bring a large pan of salted water to the boil and blanch the broccoli for 2 minutes. Remove from the water with a slotted spoon and refresh in iced water, then drain well and roughly chop. Using the same water, blanch the peas for 1 minute then refresh them in iced water and drain. Lightly crush the peas in a bowl with a fork.

Serves: 4–6
Preparation time: 35 minutes
Cooking time: around 1 hour
    40 minutes

2 courgettes, sliced diagonally into
    1cm-thick rounds
150g purple sprouting broccoli
100g fresh podded peas or petits pois
6 wild garlic leaves, finely sliced
    (optional)
12–14 sheets dried egg lasagne
250g buffalo mozzarella, thinly sliced
100g grated Cheddar cheese
sea salt and freshly ground black
    pepper

FOR THE TOMATO SAUCE
4 tbsp vegetable oil
2 onions, thinly sliced
2 garlic cloves, crushed
800g tomato passata or 2 × 400g tins
    chopped tomatoes
2 tbsp tomato purée
4 tbsp balsamic vinegar
4 tbsp Worcestershire sauce
100ml Vegetable Stock (page 57)

Preheat the oven to 200°C/180°C fan/gas 6. To assemble the lasagne, put a layer of vegetables in the base of a large ovenproof dish (approximately 20 x 30cm), add the wild garlic leaves (if using) and cover with tomato sauce. Sit a layer of pasta sheets on top, pour over a layer of white sauce and add a few slices of mozzarella. Continue with the same process, adding three layers of pasta and finishing with a layer of white sauce and mozzarella. Finally, scatter with the Cheddar, sit the dish on a baking tray and bake for about 40 minutes, until the top is golden brown.

FOR THE WHITE SAUCE
600ml whole milk
1 small onion, peeled but left whole
10 cloves
1 bay leaf
50g butter
50g plain flour

This new twist on pizza is a great dish for a summer lunch or early evening supper. Making the flatbreads from scratch is well worth it. Try different toppings, too, depending on the season and what you have in your fridge. You can also make up a load of bases and freeze them between baking parchment (pre-proving).

ROASTED RED PEPPER, ROCKET, CASHEW AND FETA FLATBREADS

To make the flatbread dough, put the flour in a large bowl, stir in the yeast, sugar, olive oil and 130–150ml of warm water and mix together to form a soft, smooth dough that leaves the sides of the bowl. Turn it out of the bowl and knead it for 7–10 minutes. Alternatively, make the dough in a standmixer fitted with a dough hook.

Transfer the dough to a clean, lightly oiled bowl, cover with oiled clingfilm and leave in a warm place for about 1 hour, or until the dough has doubled in size.

Tip the risen dough out onto a floured work surface. Cut it into 4 equal pieces and roll each piece out to an oval approximately 25cm in length. Place each dough circle on a piece of floured baking parchment and stack them on top of each other on a baking tray. Cover lightly with clingfilm and leave in a warm place to prove for 20 minutes.

Preheat the oven to 200°C/180°C fan/gas 6.

To make the dressing, whisk all of the ingredients together in a bowl, adding a little water if necessary to give the dressing a drizzling consistency. Season to taste.

Heat a large, non-stick frying pan over medium heat. When hot, add one of the flatbreads and dry-fry it for 2 ½–3½ minutes on each side until they are lightly golden and puffed up. Remove from the pan and place on a baking tray and repeat with the remaining three flatbreads.

Sprinkle the flatbreads with the chopped red pepper, cashew nuts and feta. Bake for around 10 minutes then remove from the oven and drizzle the hot flatbreads liberally with the dressing. Scatter over the rocket to serve.

Makes: 4 flatbreads
Preparation time: 30 minutes, plus 1 hour rising and 20 minutes proving
Cooking time: around 30 minutes

160g roasted red peppers, deseeded and skin removed, or piquillo peppers (jarred or tinned), drained and roughly chopped
50g cashew nuts, toasted and roughly chopped
100g feta cheese, crumbled
40g rocket
sea salt and freshly ground black pepper

FOR THE FLATBREAD DOUGH
250g strong white bread flour, plus extra for dusting
½ 7g sachet fast-action dried yeast or easy-bake yeast
½ tsp caster sugar
2 tbsp olive oil, plus extra for greasing and drizzling
½ tsp table salt

FOR THE DRESSING
2 tbsp tahini
3 tbsp Greek yoghurt
1 tbsp toasted sesame oil
1 tbsp sriracha sauce (hot chilli sauce)
1 tbsp chopped coriander
grated zest and juice of 1 lime

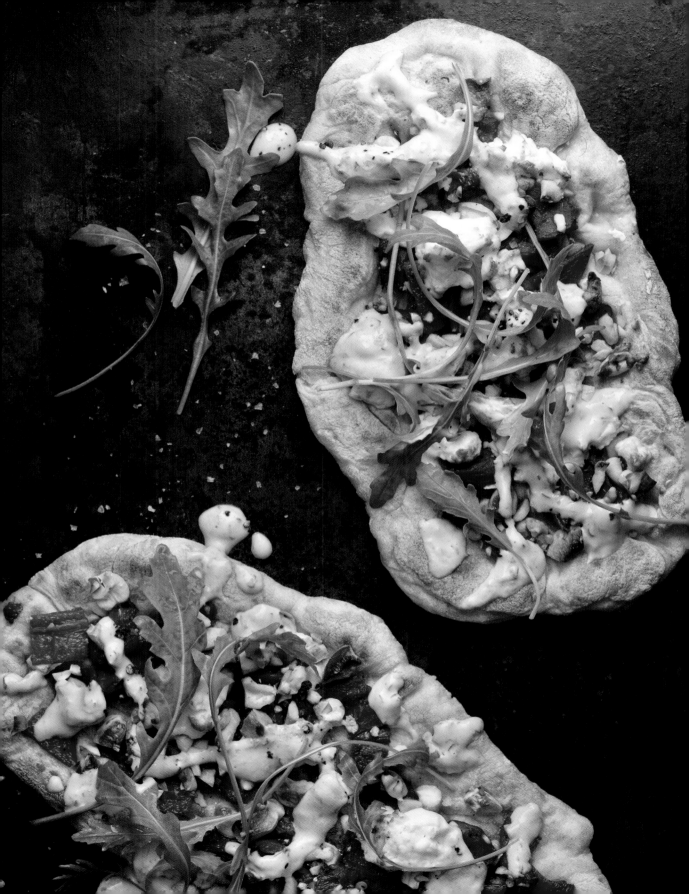

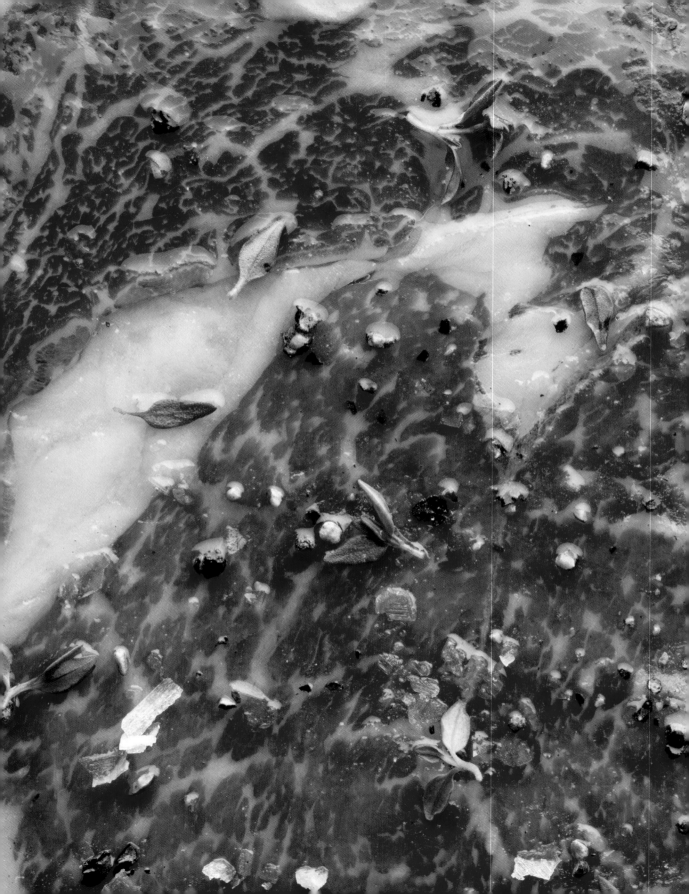

FROM THE FARM

This is a great 'go to' modern version of chicken salad that works well
for lunch or a light summer supper. Grilled gem lettuce is a perfect
accompaniment – the smoky sweetness adds even more flavour to the salad.

ROAST CHICKEN, SEMI-DRIED TOMATO, GRILLED GEM LETTUCE AND BASIL SALAD

Preheat the oven to 200°C/180°C fan/gas 6.

Lay the chicken breasts on a roasting tray, skin side up. Drizzle with the
semi-dried tomato oil and season with sea salt and pepper. Bake for
20 minutes, or until the chicken juices run clear and the skin is crisp.
Remove from the oven, covered loosely in foil, and set aside to rest.

To make the vinaigrette, whisk all of the ingredients together in a bowl and
season to taste with sea salt and pepper.

Heat a large griddle pan until almost smoking. Brush the gem wedges
with the olive oil and season them with sea salt and pepper. Grill the gem
wedges, in batches, on each cut side, for about 2 minutes, until they begin
to wilt slightly. Remove from the pan and set aside.

Assemble the grilled gem lettuce wedges on a serving platter, slice the
chicken then place it on top, along with the semi-dried tomatoes and basil
leaves. Drizzle with the vinaigrette and serve.

Serves: 2–4
Preparation time: 10 minutes
Cooking time: 20 minutes

2 boneless chicken breasts, skin on
    (about 220g each)
100g semi-dried tomatoes (from a
    jar or supermarket deli section),
    sliced, and 1 tbsp of the oil
2 baby gem lettuces, quartered
1 tbsp olive oil
½ bunch of basil, leaves picked
sea salt and freshly ground black
    pepper

FOR THE VINAIGRETTE
2 tbsp white wine vinegar
1 tsp runny honey
100ml extra virgin olive oil
1 tsp Dijon mustard
1 tsp wholegrain mustard

This recipe is great all year round. It goes really well with any meat, and also more robust fish dishes. Try it with lamb chops or grilled chicken breasts for a simple, tasty dinner. Onion seeds add a lovely savouriness to any dish, so do keep a packet in your cupboard.

GREEN BEAN, CRISPY BACON, SHALLOT AND ONION SEED SALAD

Put the butter in a deep frying pan and melt over medium-high heat. When hot, add the sliced shallots, season with sea salt, reduce the heat to medium-low and cook gently for 15–20 minutes, stirring frequently, until the shallots begin to turn a golden brown.

Meanwhile, bring a large pan of salted water to the boil, add the green beans and blanch them for 3–4 minutes. Drain and rinse under cold running water, until cool. Set aside.

Add the onion seeds and bacon to the shallots and cook gently for a further 10 minutes, until the bacon is slightly golden. Add the balsamic vinegar and cook for a further 5 minutes.

Add the beans to the pan along with the olive oil. Mix well, then remove from the heat. Taste and season with more sea salt if required, then serve.

Serves: 4
Preparation time: 15 minutes
Cooking time: 35 minutes

25g butter
8 shallots, thinly sliced
300g green beans, stalks removed
1 tbsp onion seeds
8 streaky bacon rashers, cut into
    1cm dice
2 tbsp balsamic vinegar
2 tbsp olive oil
sea salt

This is comfort food at its best. It is a great soup to take out in a flask, on a cold winter's day. I take it when I watch my sons play rugby, to have after their match – it instantly warms me from the inside out. The Marmite really enhances the savouriness of the soup, too.

CHICKEN, BARLEY AND THYME SOUP

Place the chicken, carrot, celery, onion, bay leaves, Marmite and three-quarters of the thyme in a large saucepan. Add enough cold water to cover the chicken.

Bring to the boil over high heat, skimming off any scum that rises to the surface with a spoon, then reduce the heat and leave to simmer uncovered for 1 hour. Carefully strain off the liquid into a separate large saucepan. Allow the chicken to cool slightly then, using two forks or your hands, remove all of the meat, discarding the skin and bones.

Add the barley to the chicken cooking liquid. Place over high heat and bring to the boil, then reduce the heat to a gentle simmer. Cook for 40 minutes or until the barley is almost cooked through. Add the leeks and chicken to the saucepan with the remaining thyme leaves picked from the stems. Simmer for a further 5 minutes. Remove from the heat and season generously with sea salt and add a good dose of black pepper.

Serves: 6
Preparation time: 10 minutes
Cooking time: 2 hours 40 minutes

1 whole chicken (about 1.7kg), giblets removed
2 carrots, quartered
2 celery sticks, quartered
2 onions, quartered
2 bay leaves
2 tbsp Marmite
1 bunch of thyme
200g pearl barley, rinsed
2 leeks, white part only, rinsed and finely chopped
sea salt and freshly ground black pepper

Nut butters have progressed from their humble beginnings as peanut butter and are a wonderful way of bringing flavour into a dish. They can be made with any nuts by roasting then blending them with a little oil. This is a perfect recipe for a winter dinner party, as a starter. To make a great vegetarian soup, just leave out the bacon.

BACON AND SWEET POTATO SOUP WITH ALMOND BUTTER

Preheat the oven to 200°C/180°C fan/gas 6.

Put the sweet potato chunks, roughly chopped onion, bay leaves, celery and stock in a large saucepan. Season well with sea salt and pepper then bring to the boil over high heat. Reduce the heat, cover and leave to simmer for 20–25 minutes, or until the sweet potato is soft and falling apart.

Meanwhile, heat the vegetable oil in a frying pan over medium heat. Add the finely sliced onion and bacon and cook for about 15 minutes until golden, stirring frequently.

Put the flaked almonds in a roasting tin and bake for 8–10 minutes, until dark golden, shaking the tin halfway through. Remove from the oven, tip the almonds into a blender with the olive oil, and blitz until they reach the consistency of chunky peanut butter. Season well.

Remove the bay leaves from the soup, then blend the soup in batches in a blender, or use a stick blender, until it is completely smooth. Whisk in the milk then set aside.

Add most of the bacon and onion to the soup, reserving some to serve, and bring it back to a gentle simmer. Mix well then taste and add a little more sea salt, if needed, and a good dose of black pepper.

To serve, ladle the soup into bowls. Finish with a good dollop of the almond butter and garnish with thyme leaves and the reserved bacon and onion mixture.

Serves: 6–8 (makes just over 3 litres)
Preparation time: 15 minutes
Cooking time: 20–25 minutes

4 large sweet potatoes (around 400g each), peeled and roughly chopped into 2cm chunks
2 onions, 1 roughly chopped and 1 finely sliced
2 bay leaves
2 celery sticks, chopped
2 litres Chicken Stock or Vegetable Stock (pages 83 and 57)
2 tbsp vegetable oil
200g smoked back bacon rashers, or smoked streaky bacon, diced
100g flaked almonds
3 tbsp olive oil
250ml milk or coconut milk
sea salt and freshly ground black pepper
thyme leaves, to serve

This salad sings of summer – the season when fresh peas, broad beans and goats' curd are all at their prime. Combined, the peas and beans create a fresh and crisp salad, complemented perfectly with the creamy goats' curd. If you cannot find fresh goats' curd then a soft goats' cheese will work well.

BUTTER-POACHED CHICKEN WITH PEAS, BROAD BEANS AND GOATS' CURD

Beat the butter in a bowl with the thyme leaves and season generously with sea salt and pepper. Spread the thyme butter liberally over the chicken breasts, then place each one on a separate piece of clingfilm, with a bay leaf on top, and wrap them into sausage shapes, tying the clingfilm with kitchen string at each end (or with twisted pieces of clingfilm used like string) to make the parcels watertight.

Fill a medium saucepan full of water and place over medium heat until it reaches approximately 65°C (you will see a few small bubbles, but there will be no movement of water in the pan). Place the chicken breasts in the water and poach gently for 20 minutes.

While the chicken is poaching, bring a large pan of salted water to the boil and blanch the broad beans for 3 minutes. Drain and rinse under cold running water until cool. Drain again thoroughly. Remove the broad beans from their skins by squeezing them between your thumb and index finger.

Mix the peas, sugar snaps, broad beans and most of the pea shoots together in a bowl. Place the goats' curd in a bowl with the lemon zest and season with sea salt and pepper. Mix well.

Whisk the lemon juice with the olive oil and season lightly.

When the chicken has finished poaching, remove both breasts from the water and carefully open the clingfilm over a bowl, retaining all of the juices that escape so that they can be drizzled over the top. Slice the chicken.

Place the pea and bean mix on a large platter and drizzle the lemon juice and olive oil over the top. Dollop the goats' curd around the salad and top with the sliced chicken, cooking juices and the remaining pea shoots. Serve immediately.

Serves: 4
Preparation time: 15 minutes
Cooking time: 20 minutes

100g soft butter
4 sprigs of thyme, leaves picked
2 skinless, boneless chicken breasts
2 bay leaves
100g broad beans
100g fresh peas, podded
100g sugar snap peas, finely sliced
50g pea shoots
150g goats' curd
finely grated zest and juice of
    ½ lemon
50ml olive oil
sea salt and freshly ground black
    pepper

Chicken liver pâté is one of my all-time favourite things. It is simple to make at home, but you need to work quickly, to ensure it stays a lovely pink colour and avoid it oxidising and turning brown. The lapsang souchong adds a lovely smoky flavour to the pâté.

CHICKEN LIVER PÂTÉ WITH GINGER AND LAPSANG SOUCHONG JELLY

Get your food processor ready and place an oval pie dish (approximately 18cm in length) in the fridge to chill. Prepare a large bowl of iced water.

Wash the chicken livers under cold running water and pat them dry with kitchen paper. Trim off any sinew and cut larger livers in half.

Add 2 tablespoons of the butter in a large frying pan over medium heat. When hot, add the shallots and thyme, season well with sea salt, and cook for 5–7 minutes until soft and golden. Add the wine and cook for 3–4 minutes until reduced by half. Remove the thyme and place the mix in the food processor.

Add 2 more tablespoons of butter to the frying pan. Place over high heat and when hot, season the livers and fry them in two batches for about 1 minute each side, until golden but not cooked through. Add them to the food processor and blend. Pour the remaining melted butter into the food processor and blend until smooth. Taste and season if necessary. Pass the paste through a fine sieve into a bowl on top of the bowl of iced water. Whisk the pâté until it starts to cool then place in the pie dish, cover with clingfilm and chill.

Bring 150ml water to the boil in a pan and add the tea. Remove from the heat and cover with clingfilm. Leave to infuse for 10 minutes. While the tea leaves are infusing, soak the gelatine leaves in a bowl of cold water for 5 minutes.

Strain the tea into a clean saucepan and add the ginger wine. Bring back to the boil then remove from the heat. Squeeze the gelatine leaves to remove excess water and whisk into the tea and ginger wine. Pass through a fine sieve into a heatproof bowl. Place the bowl on top of the larger bowl filled with iced water. Allow to cool a little until tepid, then pour it over the pâté. Chill the pâté for at least 2 hours, or until it is completely cold and has set. Serve with crusty bread and pickles.

Serves: 4–6
Preparation time: 20 minutes, plus minimum 2 hours chilling
Cooking time: 15 minutes

400g chicken livers
200g butter, melted
4 shallots, finely sliced
¼ bunch of thyme
60ml green ginger wine

FOR THE LAPSANG SOUCHONG JELLY
1 tsp lapsang souchong tea
2 gelatine leaves
50ml green ginger wine
sea salt and freshly ground black pepper

BRINING

Brining means to soak an ingredient in a salt solution. It can be used to preserve ingredients, or, as in this case, it seasons the meat all the way through, rather than just on the outside (when you season a piece of meat just before adding to the pan). It is a technique I use both in the restaurants and at home, for many cuts of meat. I generally work on a 7% salt ratio for brining meat.

Allowing meat to marinate in salted water enhances its flavour. As well as providing seasoning, the salt causes the proteins in the flesh to relax, making the meat juicier and more tender as a result.

You can also brine fish and vegetables but because they generally have a higher water content I find that using rock salt in its raw form is a better way to distribute the seasoning throughout the produce (see Salt and Pepper Plaice, page 184).

Using herbs and spices also adds to the flavour. I like to include peppercorns, fennel seeds, coriander seeds, thyme and bay leaves in my brines, but do feel free to experiment with your favourite herbs and spices, in moderation.

The time it takes to brine a piece of meat depends on its size. For example, brining a whole chicken will take much longer than brining a chicken thigh, so follow the quantities and timings below. It is important not to leave the meat for too long in the brine, otherwise you run the risk that the meat will be too salty, and the proteins begin to break down, thus affecting the structure of the meat.

MEAT BRINE

Put all the ingredients in a saucepan. Add 500ml warm water and bring to the boil. Simmer for 2 minutes then remove from the heat and add 500ml cold water. Allow to cool completely then place the meat in a container, add the brine, ensuring the meat is completely covered, and transfer to the fridge for the time shown in the table below. When ready to cook, remove the meat from the brining liquid, rinse it well under cold running water, pat it dry with kitchen paper and let it come to room temperature.

70g table salt
¼ tsp white peppercorns
¼ tsp coriander seeds
¼ tsp fennel seeds
3 sprigs of thyme
1 bay leaf

MEAT	MEAT BRINE QUANTITY	BRINING TIME
Whole chicken	2–3 quantities (depending on the size of the bird)	24 hours
Chicken breast, duck breasts	1 quantity	2 hours
Beef steaks, lamb rumps	2 quantities	2 hours
Small joints of beef, pork or lamb	2 quantities	2 hours
Large joints of beef, pork or lamb	3 quantities	3 hours

This chicken, smothered in rosemary butter, smells amazing while roasting. The brining of the chicken really does enhance the flavour and texture, so do give it a try. The baked fennel also works well with it, as when it's roasted it takes on a lovely sweetness. This dish is a one-pot wonder, making washing up a little easier.

ROSEMARY ROAST CHICKEN WITH BAKED FENNEL AND POTATOES

Preheat the oven to 220°C/200°C fan/gas 7 and lightly grease a large roasting tray.

Mix the butter in a bowl with the garlic, a generous pinch each of sea salt and pepper and the chopped rosemary until well combined. Rinse the chicken under cold running water and pat it dry with kitchen paper. Use your hands to smear two-thirds of the flavoured butter under the skin of the chicken and all over the flesh of the breasts and legs. Smear the remaining third over the top of the chicken.

Season the cavity and the outside of the bird with a little more sea salt and pepper. Sit the chicken in the greased roasting tray and roast it in the oven for 20 minutes until it starts to take on a golden colour. Remove from the oven and reduce the oven temperature to 200°C/180°C fan/gas 6. Add the potatoes, fennel seeds and rosemary sprigs to the roasting tray, season well and place back in the oven.

Continue to roast for a further 30 minutes. Turn the potatoes, then add the fennel to the roasting tray and place back in the oven for a further 15 minutes, turning the fennel halfway through. To check the chicken is cooked, insert a skewer into the thickest part of the thigh – if the juices run clear it is ready. If not, continue to cook for a further 15–20 minutes and test again. Remove the chicken, fennel and potatoes from the tray to a large dish. Loosely cover with foil and leave to rest for 5 minutes.

Serves: 4–6
Preparation time: 15 minutes, plus 12–24 hours brining
Cooking time: about 1 hour 15 minutes (or longer, depending on the size of your chicken)

50g soft butter
2 garlic cloves, finely grated
1 bunch of rosemary, ½ of the needles finely chopped
1 x 1.4–1.8kg large chicken (giblets removed), brined (page 77)
4 large King Edward or Chippies Choice or other floury potatoes, scrubbed and cut into large wedges
½ tsp fennel seeds, crushed
1 fennel bulb, cut into 1cm-thick slices
300ml Chicken Stock (page 83)
2 tbsp double cream
sea salt and freshly ground black pepper

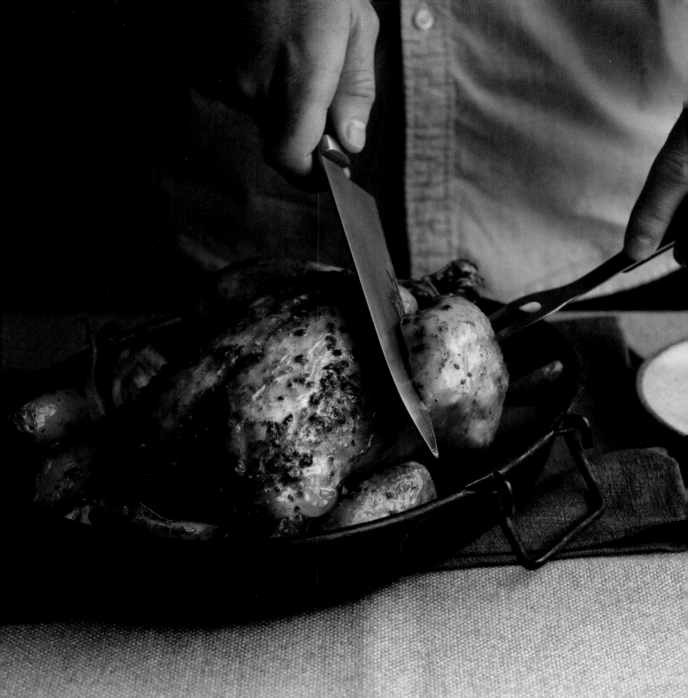

Put the roasting tray directly on the hob over medium heat and stir in the stock. Bring to the boil and simmer for 5 minutes. Pass the gravy through a sieve to remove the rosemary sprigs then whisk in the double cream and season to taste.

Carve the chicken and serve it with the fennel, potatoes and gravy.

Hanger, or onglet, is a very tender cut of meat that literally hangs between the fillet and the rib. I highly recommend brining this cut of meat as it not only seasons it but also tenderises it slightly, ensuring it melts in the mouth when cooked.

HANGER STEAK WITH SAUCE GRIBICHE AND CONFIT EGG YOLK

To make the confit egg yolk, fill a medium saucepan with hot water and place the eggs in the pan. Using a thermometer, heat the water to 65°C. Keep the water between 60 and 65°C for 45 minutes. Remove the eggs and leave them to cool for about 1 hour at room temperature. Peel the shell off, as well as the white, and the membrane around the egg yolk. Place the confit egg yolks in a bowl and whisk them together for 3 minutes until smooth. Season to taste and set aside.

Preheat the oven to 200°C/180°C fan/gas 6.

To make the sauce gribiche, mix all ingredients together in a bowl and season with sea salt to taste.

Heat a griddle pan over high heat until very hot. Rinse the steaks under cold running water and pat them dry with kitchen paper. Brush the steaks all over with a little olive oil. Sear them on the griddle for about 3 minutes, turning them until they are nicely charred all over. Place on a roasting tray or ovenproof frying pan and place in the oven for 4–5 minutes (for medium-rare doneness). Remove from the oven and transfer to a plate. Cover loosely with foil and leave to rest for 5 minutes.

Carve the steaks and serve them with a good dollop each of the egg yolk and sauce gribiche.

Serves: 4
Preparation time: 15 minutes, plus
    2 hours brining and 1 hour cooling
Cooking time: about 55 minutes

6 eggs
4 hanger (or onglet) steaks (approx.
    200–250g each), brined (page 77)
olive oil, for brushing
sea salt and freshly ground black
    pepper

FOR THE SAUCE GRIBICHE
50g capers, finely chopped
50g gherkins, finely chopped
1 shallot, finely diced
½ bunch of tarragon, chopped
½ bunch of flat-leaf parsley, chopped
4 tbsp good-quality mayonnaise
4 tbsp crème fraîche

Coq au Vin is a classic French casserole, using a rooster (cockerel) and lashings of red wine. My twist on this classic is to use chicken thighs rather than a whole jointed bird as there is more flavour in the thighs. It is a perfect winter comfort food. Start this recipe the day before you want to serve it, to allow for marinating time. This is one of those dishes which will be even more delicious if you use homemade stock.

COQ AU VIN

Put all ingredients for the chicken marinade in a large pan and bring to the boil. Simmer rapidly for 10 minutes, then remove from the heat and leave to cool completely.

Place the chicken pieces in a large non-reactive container then pour over the cooled liquid. Leave in the fridge to marinate for a minimum of 24 hours, maximum of 36 hours.

Remove the chicken pieces from the marinade and pat them dry with kitchen paper. Strain off the vegetables and reserve them separately to the liquid.

Heat 2 tablespoons of the duck fat or butter in a large pan over high heat and, when hot, add the vegetables from the marinade. Cook for 10–15 minutes until they are a darkened. Deglaze with the brandy then add the reserved marinade liquid. Bring to the boil and simmer rapidly for about 15 minutes, until the marinade has become a syrup. Add the chicken stock and simmer gently for a further 15 minutes.

Preheat the oven to 180°C/160°C fan/gas 4.

Mix the flour with the table salt and pepper.

Heat a large frying pan with another 2 tablespoons of the duck fat or butter over medium-high heat. When hot, dust the chicken pieces all over with the seasoned flour and fry them in batches – 10 minutes for each batch – adding another tablespoons of duck fat if needed, until golden brown.

Serves: 4–6
Preparation time: 20 minutes, plus at least 24 hours marinating
Cooking time: 2 hours 20 minutes

8 bone-in, skin-on, chicken thighs or 1 whole large chicken, jointed into 8 pieces
4–5 tbsp duck fat or butter
2 tbsp brandy
500ml Chicken Stock (page 83)
4 tbsp plain flour
½ tsp table salt
½ tsp freshly ground black pepper
250g smoked streaky bacon, cut into 1cm-long lardons
250g button mushrooms, quartered
200g small shallots, peeled
½ bunch of flat-leaf parsley, leaves chopped

Place the chicken in a large casserole dish and set aside. Keeping the fat in the frying pan, add the bacon and fry for 5–7 minutes until well browned, stirring frequently. Add the bacon to the chicken. Add the mushrooms to the frying pan and cook for 7 minutes until well browned, add them to the chicken, then cook the shallots in the pan for 7 minutes and add them to the chicken, too. Leave any fat behind in the pan.

Strain the sauce through a fine sieve and pour on top of the chicken, lardons, mushrooms and onions. Cover and place in the oven for 40–50 minutes, until the juices run clear from the chicken when pricked with a knife into the thickest part of a thigh. Stir in the parsley and serve.

FOR THE CHICKEN MARINADE
750ml red wine (I prefer malbec or merlot)
4 tbsp sweet sherry
2 carrots, chopped
2 celery sticks, quartered
1 onion, chopped
4 garlic cloves, finely grated
½ bunch of thyme
3 bay leaves
½ tsp table salt
½ tsp freshly ground black pepper

CHICKEN STOCK

Put the chicken carcasses in a large stock pot and cover with 4 litres of water. Bring to the boil and, once boiling, skim the surface to remove any discoloured foam/scum.

Reduce the heat to a simmer, then add the remaining ingredients. Leave to simmer for 2–3 hours over low heat, adding more water if the liquid reduces by more than two-thirds.

Skim off any discoloured foam throughout cooking. Strain the stock through a colander and then through a fine sieve.

Use the stock straight away or keep in the fridge for 3–4 days, removing any surface fat before using. Alternatively, freeze and use within 4 months.

Makes: approx. 2 litres
Preparation time: 10 minutes
Cooking time: 2–3 hours

2 raw chicken carcasses, each cut into 4 pieces
2 onions, chopped
2 leeks, white part only, chopped
2 celery sticks, chopped
¼ bunch of thyme
2 bay leaves
½ tsp white peppercorns

Miso is a wonderful ingredient that is very useful as a seasoning. It adds a lovely savouriness to any dish. It is widely available these days and has a long shelf life, so is always handy to have in the fridge. This recipe calls for marinating the thighs in advance, as well as soaking the sticky rice, but putting in the effort ahead of time is well worth it.

MISO-GLAZED CHICKEN THIGHS WITH STICKY RICE AND SESAME GREENS

Put the rice in a bowl, cover it with water and leave it to soak for at least 6 hours (up to 12 hours).

Whisk the ingredients for the marinade together in a bowl with 2 tablespoons of warm water. Put the chicken thighs in a glass or metal container (non-reactive) then coat them liberally with the marinade. Cover and chill in the fridge for at least 6 hours (up to 12 hours).

Preheat your grill. Cover a large roasting tray with foil and arrange the marinated chicken thighs right side up. Place under the grill for 12–15 minutes, basting them twice during the cooking time. They will become golden and sticky.

Meanwhile, fill a saucepan that fits your steamer a third full with water and bring to the boil. Drain the soaked rice and place it in a steamer over the saucepan. Cover and steam for 15 minutes until cooked through and fluffy.

While the chicken is cooking, trim the ends off the pak choi and cut each head in quarters. Heat the sesame oil in a large, deep frying pan with a lid. Season the pak choi, place them the hot oil and brown on all sides, then add the sesame seeds and cook for a further 3 minutes. Add a splash of water and place the lid on top. Turn off the heat and leave to sit for 5 minutes to cook through.

Serve the thighs with the sticky rice and sesame pak choi.

Serves: 4
Preparation time: 15 minutes, plus 6–12 hours soaking and marinating
Cooking time: 25–30 minutes

250g Thai sticky rice
8 skinless and boneless chicken thighs
300g pak choi (2 heads)
2 tbsp toasted sesame oil
1 tbsp sesame seeds
sea salt and freshly ground black pepper

FOR THE MARINADE
4 tbsp white miso paste
grated zest and juice of 1 lime
2 tbsp toasted sesame oil
1 tbsp runny honey
½ tsp coriander seeds, lightly crushed with a rolling pin

This is one of my favourite dishes in the book, and it brings something new to the familiar flavours of chicken pie. It's a wonderful dish to make in advance. Just make the scones when you are ready to bake it. This is pure comfort food and works well all year round. Try it instead of a traditional Sunday roast. It would also work well made with leftover turkey on Boxing Day, rather than chicken. *See image on following pages.*

CHICKEN, MUSTARD AND SPINACH COBBLER

Preheat the oven to 200°C/180°C fan/gas 6.

Lay a sheet of foil on your work surface. Place the chicken breasts, butter and a generous pinch of sea salt and pepper on top then gather the foil around it. Place the foil package on a baking tray and bake in the oven for 15 minutes. Remove and allow to cool in the foil for 20 minutes, then unwrap and roughly chop the chicken.

Meanwhile, make the scones. Mix together the 175g flour, baking powder, grated Cheddar, herbs, fine salt and pepper in a bowl. When combined, rub in the grated butter with your fingers, until it is well dispersed (the mixture will have a fine crumb texture). Add just enough cold water (3–4 tablespoons) to bring the crumbs together to form a dough, taking care not to overmix, as this will make the scones tough. Form the dough into a ball, wrap it in clingfilm and place it in the fridge for at least 20 minutes.

Bring a large pan of salted water to the boil and blanch the spinach leaves for 1 minute. Refresh in iced water, until cool, then drain well. Squeeze out the excess water with your hands, a handful at a time. Roughly chop the spinach and set it aside.

Serves: 4
Preparation time: 25 minutes, plus
    about 40 minutes resting
Cooking time: 40 minutes, plus
    5 minutes resting

3 skinless chicken breasts
25g butter
250g baby spinach
1 egg, beaten
sea salt and freshly ground black
    pepper

FOR THE SCONES
175g self-raising flour, plus extra for
    dusting
1 tsp baking powder
30g grated Cheddar cheese
1 tbsp finely chopped tarragon
1 tbsp finely chopped flat-leaf parsley
½ tsp fine salt
½ tsp freshly ground black pepper
100g cold butter, grated

While the scone dough is resting in the fridge, make the white sauce. Melt the butter in a medium saucepan and when it starts bubbling whisk in the flour. Cook for 30 seconds, stirring, then gradually whisk in the milk and stock, a little at a time. When all the milk and stock have been added, bring the sauce to a gentle simmer and cook for 10 minutes, whisking regularly to prevent it catching on the bottom of the pan. Remove from the heat, add both mustards, the Worcestershire sauce and season with sea salt. Add the chicken and spinach and mix well.

Remove the scone dough from the fridge and unwrap it. Dust the work surface with flour and roll out the scone dough to a thickness of 2cm, then cover it loosely with clingfilm and leave it to rest for 20 minutes.

Put the chicken and spinach mix in an ovenproof dish (approximately 30 x 30cm) or four individual dishes (approximately 15cm in diameter). Cut out 25–30 rounds of scone dough, about 4–5cm in diameter, and place them on top of the chicken mix, without overlapping them. Brush the scones with the beaten egg. Bake for 20–25 minutes until the scones are golden and the chicken mix is bubbling.

FOR THE WHITE SAUCE
60g butter
60g plain flour
300ml milk
300ml Chicken Stock (page 83)
1 tbsp Dijon mustard
2 tbsp wholegrain mustard
2 tbsp Worcestershire sauce

This was one of my favourite dishes when I was growing up. We would not eat out often, but when we did, I loved chicken and cashew stir-fry. The chicken was so tender, which always puzzled me. When I spoke to a chef years later I found out that the secret was marinating it in bicarbonate of soda.

CHICKEN, CASHEW AND BEANSPROUT STIR-FRY

Put the chicken pieces and bicarbonate of soda in a bowl, mix evenly, then cover the bowl with clingfilm and set aside for 15 minutes.

Rinse the chicken pieces thoroughly under cold running water then pat them dry with kitchen paper.

To make the sauce, put all ingredients in a bowl and whisk them together. Combine half of the sauce with the chicken and set aside to marinate for 30 minutes.

Whisk the cornflour in a bowl with 6 tablespoons of cold water. Whisk this into the remaining sauce.

Heat the vegetable oil in a large lidded frying pan or wok over high heat. When almost smoking, add the onion and stir-fry until golden brown. Add the garlic and stir-fry for 1 minute until brown, then add the marinated chicken and cook for a further 3 minutes. Add the rest of the sauce and mix well, add the broccoli florets and cover with a lid. Let it steam for 3 minutes, or until the chicken is cooked through.

Remove the lid and stir in the cashew nuts, bean sprouts and coriander to finish. Serve with egg noodles or steamed white rice.

Serves: 4
Preparation time: 15 minutes, plus 45 minutes marinating
Cooking time: 10 minutes

600g boneless chicken breasts or thighs, cut into medium chunks
2 tsp bicarbonate of soda
1 tbsp cornflour
2 tbsp vegetable oil
1 onion, finely sliced
2 garlic cloves, grated
1 broccoli head, cut into little florets
150g roasted cashew nuts
150g mung bean sprouts
2 tbsp finely chopped coriander leaves
egg noodles or steamed white rice, to serve

FOR THE SAUCE
4 tbsp dark soy sauce
2 tbsp toasted sesame oil
2 tbsp dry sherry
2 tbsp oyster sauce
1 tsp rice wine vinegar

My family always enjoys my version of this classic dish. Making your own spice mixes, though more time consuming, is very rewarding. You can also tweak them to include more of the things you really like, or to have more or less heat. Do ensure your spices are fresh, however. You don't want to use them if they've been stuck at the back of your cupboard for years!

CHICKEN TIKKA MASALA

To make the marinade, heat a dry frying pan over medium heat. Add the cumin seeds, coriander seeds, mustard seeds, paprika and garam masala and stir over the heat for 3–5 minutes, until fragrant and the seeds begin to pop. Transfer the toasted spices to a pestle and mortar, or a spice grinder, and crush the spice mix until it forms a powder. Mix with the remaining marinade ingredients in a bowl, add the chicken pieces and coat them well. Place in a glass or metal container (that won't get stained or tainted by the marinade), cover and chill for 6–12 hours.

To make the masala sauce (you can make this in advance and chill until needed, if you wish), heat the oil in a frying pan over medium heat. Add the onions and table salt and fry for 10–15 minutes until the onions are soft and translucent. Add the garlic and ginger and cook for a few more minutes until soft, then add the turmeric and chilli and cook for a further 4 minutes. Add the tomato paste and mix well, then stir in the stock. Tie the coriander stalks together with kitchen string and add them to the pan. Leave to simmer gently for 20 minutes, stirring occasionally.

Meanwhile, heat a griddle pan over high heat. Remove the marinated chicken from the fridge and fry it on the griddle, in small batches. Once the meat is golden brown, flip it over to colour the other side.

Remove the coriander stalks from the masala sauce and add the grilled chicken pieces. Simmer very gently for a further 10–15 minutes until the chicken is cooked through. Season with salt and pepper to taste, finish with the yoghurt and coriander leaves and serve with rice and naan bread.

Serves: 4–6
Preparation time: 20 minutes, plus
    6–12 hours marinating
Cooking time: 50 minutes

8 skinless and boneless chicken
    thighs, cut into 3cm chunks
sea salt and freshly ground black
    pepper

FOR THE MARINADE
1 tsp cumin seeds
1 tsp coriander seeds
1 tsp yellow mustard seeds
1 tsp paprika
1 tsp garam masala
2cm piece of root ginger, peeled and
    grated
2 garlic cloves, crushed
finely grated zest and juice of ½ lemon
3 tbsp Greek yoghurt
2 tbsp vegetable oil
1 tsp table salt

FOR THE MASALA SAUCE
4 tbsp vegetable oil
2 onions, finely sliced
1 tsp table salt
4 garlic cloves, crushed
3cm piece of root ginger, peeled and
    finely grated
½ tsp ground turmeric
1 red chilli, deseeded and finely
    chopped
2 tbsp tomato paste
350ml Chicken Stock (page 83)
½ bunch of coriander, stalks reserved
    and leaves roughly chopped
3 tbsp Greek yoghurt
rice and naan bread, to serve

This is a great summer dish which, once the preparation is done the day before, is very quick to cook and serve. The chicken and pickled lettuce are also delicious served on a baguette or in pitta bread for a lighter lunch.

CRISPY CHICKEN THIGHS WITH PEANUT AND COCONUT SAUCE AND PICKLED LETTUCE

Serves: 4
Preparation time: 15 minutes, plus
    12–24 hours marinating
Cooking time: about 35 minutes

8 bone-in, skin-on, chicken thighs
1 iceberg lettuce head, finely shredded
1 tbsp finely chopped coriander
steamed white rice, to serve

FOR THE PEANUT AND
COCONUT SAUCE
2 tbsp vegetable oil
1 onion, finely sliced
1 garlic clove, grated
1 red chilli, deseeded and finely
    chopped
2 tbsp fish sauce
1 tbsp soft light brown sugar
½ tsp ground turmeric
100g toasted peanuts, finely chopped
1 x 400ml tin coconut milk

FOR THE PICKLING LIQUID
25g caster sugar
150ml white wine vinegar
½ tsp fish sauce
¼ tsp dried chilli flakes
½ tsp table salt

To make the peanut and coconut sauce, heat the oil in a medium frying pan over medium heat. Add the onion and fry for 10–15 minutes, stirring frequently, until golden brown. Add the garlic and chilli and cook for 2 minutes, then add the fish sauce, brown sugar, turmeric and peanuts. Cook for 2 minutes, then add the coconut milk and simmer gently for 5 minutes.

Transfer the sauce to a blender and pulse until a chunky sauce consistency is reached. Allow to cool, then place the chicken thighs in a bowl and cover them with half of the sauce. Cover and chill for a minimum of 12 hours, maximum of 24 hours. Chill the remaining sauce in a separate bowl.

To make the pickling liquid, put all ingredients in a saucepan and bring to the boil. Once the sugar has dissolved, remove from the heat and leave to cool, then chill in the fridge.

When ready to serve, preheat the oven to 220°C/200°C fan/gas 7 and line an oven tray with foil. Mix the shredded lettuce with the chopped coriander and pickling liquid and set aside. Place the marinated chicken thighs skin side down on the lined tray and bake for 15–20 minutes until golden and the juices run clear, then turn the chicken over, turn on the oven grill and grill for 5 minutes to crisp up the skin. Heat the remaining sauce in a saucepan and serve the chicken with the warm sauce, pickled lettuce and steamed white rice.

A new take on the classic Beef Wellington, these individual pastry parcels are delicious. They require some preparation but the end result is really worth it – they make an impressive dinner party main course that is so full of flavour. Brining the chicken enhances its flavour and also removes a little of the moisture that risks making the pastry soggy. I like to serve with Tenderstem broccoli and grilled courgettes. *See image on following pages.*

CHICKEN WELLINGTONS WITH MUSTARD SAUCE

To make the mushroom duxelle, heat the butter in a large frying pan over medium-high heat. When hot, add the onion and cook for about 5 minutes until translucent. Add the mushrooms, thyme leaves and table salt and continue to cook for about 10 minutes until all the moisture from the mushrooms has evaporated. Deglaze with the Madeira or sherry and cook for a further 5 minutes, again until all of the moisture has evaporated. Transfer the mushroom mixture to a bowl and chill until cold.

Bring a large pan of salted water to the boil and blanch the spinach leaves for 30 seconds. Remove them carefully and refresh in ice-cold water, then drain well and pat dry with kitchen paper.

To assemble the Wellingtons, cover your work surface with a large double layer of clingfilm and cut into 4 pieces about 30 x 35cm. Rinse the brined chicken breasts under cold running water and pat them dry with kitchen paper. Place a spinach leaf on top of each double-layered piece of clingfilm followed by a chicken breast. Divide the duxelle into four portions and spread it liberally over each chicken breast. Next, add the second spinach leaf on top of the chicken breast and wrap the two leaves around the chicken so the breasts are completely encased (you may need an extra spinach leaf). Wrap each breast tightly in the clingfilm and twist each end so it forms a sausage shape. Chill in the fridge for 30 minutes.

Serves: 4
Preparation time: 30 minutes, plus
    2 hours brining and 1 hour chilling
Cooking time: 1 hour

8–12 large spinach leaves
4 small, skinless and boneless
    chicken breasts (about 120g each),
    brined (page 77)
2 x 375g sheets of ready-rolled all-
    butter puff pastry
2 egg yolks, beaten
sea salt and freshly ground black
    pepper

FOR THE MUSHROOM DUXELLE
25g butter
1 small onion, finely diced
300g flat-cap mushrooms, finely
    diced
1 tsp thyme leaves
½ tsp table salt
2 tbsp Madeira wine or sweet sherry

Lay one sheet of puff pastry out on your work surface, roll it out slightly to make it bigger (about 1.5–2cm longer and 1.5–2cm wider), then cut it in half. Unwrap a chicken breast and place it on one of the pieces of pastry so one side is in the centre of one of the pastry halves. Wet the edges of the pastry around the chicken breast then fold the pastry over the chicken breast, sealing the edges by crimping them with a fork and removing any excess pastry. Repeat with the other 3 chicken breasts. Place the Wellingtons seam side down on a plate in the fridge for 30 minutes to chill.

Preheat the oven to 200°C/180°C fan/gas 6 and line a baking tray with baking parchment.

When ready to cook the Wellingtons, brush them liberally with egg yolk and place them seam side down on the lined baking tray. Mark small patterns or lines in the pastry with a knife, if you like, then bake for 30–35 minutes.

In the meantime, make the mustard sauce. Melt the butter in a medium saucepan over medium heat. When hot, add the onion, bay leaves and table salt, reduce the heat to low and cook gently for about 15 minutes, until golden. Deglaze the pan with the Madeira or sherry and cook for a further 3 minutes, then add the mustards and chicken stock and simmer for 20 minutes. Remove from the heat and add the cream and tarragon just before serving the Wellingtons, tasting the sauce and adding more salt and pepper if necessary.

Remove the Wellingtons from the oven and leave them to rest for 5 minutes. Slice the rested Wellingtons in half and serve them with the sauce.

FOR THE MUSTARD SAUCE

25g butter

1 onion, finely sliced

2 bay leaves

½ tsp table salt

2 tbsp Madeira or sweet sherry

1 tsp wholegrain mustard

1 tsp Dijon mustard

500ml Chicken Stock (page 83)

100ml double cream

2 tbsp finely chopped tarragon leaves

This is a great dish for late summer, when sweetcorn is at its prime and you need a little comfort food as the days begin to get shorter. If poussin are unavailable, use a corn-fed chicken and just double the meat cooking times.

ROAST POUSSIN WITH MUSHROOMS, SWEETCORN AND TARRAGON

Preheat the oven to 200°C/180°C fan/gas 6.

Mix the thyme and table salt in a bowl with half the soft butter until smooth. Loosen the poussin skin from the breast with your fingers, then spread the herb butter under the skin of each poussin. Place the birds in a shallow roasting dish and cook in the oven for 30–35 minutes, basting them with their cooking juices after 15 minutes of cooking time, until the juices run clear when a skewer or knife is inserted into the thickest part of the thigh. Remove from the oven and leave to rest, covered in foil, for 10 minutes before serving.

While the birds are cooking, bring a large saucepan of salted water to the boil. Boil the cobs of corn for 4–6 minutes until bright yellow and the corn is cooked. Drain, then place in the fridge to cool. Once cool, slice the kernels off the husks, being careful not to cut too far into the coarse husk.

Pour the chicken stock into a large saucepan, add the corn husks, bring to the boil and simmer rapidly until the liquid reduces by two-thirds. Take off the heat, remove the husks, add the lemon zest then season lightly to taste.

Wash the mushrooms thoroughly to remove any grit, then slice them into evenly-sized pieces if necessary. Heat the remaining butter in a large frying pan over medium-high heat. When hot, add the mushrooms, season well with sea salt and pepper and fry for about 10 minutes, until golden and tender. Add the sweetcorn kernels to the pan and a little of the reduced stock.

When ready to serve, add the crème fraîche and tarragon to the rest of the reduced stock. Cut each poussin in half, down the breast bone (kitchen scissors work well) and serve with the mushrooms and sweetcorn, and the chicken sauce on the side.

Serves: 4
Preparation time: 20 minutes
Cooking time: 35 minutes, plus
    10 minutes resting

1 tsp thyme leaves
½ tsp table salt
50g soft butter
2 x 400–500g poussin
4 cobs of corn
300ml Chicken Stock (page 83)
grated zest of ½ lemon
200g wild mushrooms
2 tbsp crème fraîche
2 tbsp chopped tarragon leaves
sea salt and freshly ground black
    pepper

Duck breasts are a lot easier to cook than people tend to think. Due to the large amount of fat in the skin they are best cooked slowly so the fat has a chance to render down, and the skin to crisp up. The combination of duck, tamarind, cashew and pickled plums might seem a little unusual – and a radical change from sweet cherries – but the flavours work so well together. The dish involves extended soaking and brining, making it better for weekend cooking.

DUCK WITH TAMARIND SAUCE, CASHEW BUTTER, FREEKEH AND PICKLED PLUMS

To make the cashew butter, put the cashews in a small container, cover with cold water and add the table salt. Cover and leave to soak at room temperature for 12 hours. After the 12 hours have passed, blitz the soaked cashews in a food processor or blender until smooth, adding half the soaking water. Pass the cashew butter through a fine sieve and add salt to taste.

To make the tamarind sauce, heat the vegetable oil in a large saucepan over medium-high heat. Add the carrot, shallots, garlic, ginger and star anise and fry for 4–5 minutes until well browned, stirring frequently. Deglaze with the red wine and Madeira, then reduce the heat to medium-low and simmer for 5–10 minutes until it reduces to a thick syrup. Add the remaining sauce ingredients and simmer gently for 30 minutes. Remove from the heat and pass the sauce through a fine sieve (it's a thin sauce).

Cook the freekeh according to the packet instructions, with the bay leaves added to the water.

Remove the duck breasts from the brine, rinse them under cold running water and pat them dry with kitchen paper. Score the skin on the duck breasts. Put them in a large, heavy-based frying pan, skin side down, and place the pan over medium-low heat. The fat from the skin will slowly start to render and the skin will begin to brown. Do not rush this process as this will give the breasts a crispy skin (around 20 minutes). Move the breasts around the pan and, when golden on the skin side, turn them over and cook on the other side for a few minutes. Spoon the fat over the breasts while they're cooking. When the underside is golden, remove from the pan and leave the duck to rest for 5 minutes.

Serves: 4
Preparation time: 20 minutes,
    plus 12 hours soaking and
    2 hours brining
Cooking time: 40 minutes

100g freekeh
2 bay leaves
4 boneless skin-on duck breasts,
    brined (page 77)
knob of butter
sea salt and freshly ground black
    pepper

FOR THE PICKLED PLUMS
2 plums
2 tbsp white wine vinegar

FOR THE CASHEW BUTTER
100g roasted cashew nuts, plus 20g
    extra to serve
½ tsp table salt

Make the pickled plums 15 minutes before you are ready to serve. Halve, stone and slice the plums thinly and marinate them in the vinegar.

To serve, heat the cooked freekeh through with 8 tablespoons of the tamarind sauce and the knob of butter in a saucepan. Season if necessary.

Place a spoonful of the cashew butter on each plate then top with the freekeh. Slice each duck breast into 5 pieces and place them on top of the freekeh. Heat the rest of the sauce and drizzle a little around the plate. Finish with the pickled plums and chopped cashews.

FOR THE TAMARIND SAUCE

1 tbsp vegetable oil
1 carrot, sliced
2 shallots, sliced
2 garlic cloves (unpeeled)
4cm piece of fresh ginger, sliced
2 star anise
50ml red wine
50ml Madeira
25ml soy sauce
100g tamarind concentrate
300ml Chicken Stock (page 83)

Confit duck, roasted until the skin turns deliciously crunchy, is such a wonderful thing to eat. Its richness is cut well here with the sweet acidity of pink grapefruit. This is a great midweek meal as it can be made relatively quickly if you confit the duck ahead of time, and it's delicious.

CRISPY DUCK SALAD WITH PINK GRAPEFRUIT, CASHEW AND CORIANDER

Start by confiting the duck. Lay the duck legs, skin side up, in a shallow bowl or tray. Sprinkle over the rock salt and leave in the fridge for about 4 hours.

Rinse the salt from the duck legs and pat them dry with kitchen paper.

Preheat the oven to 150°C/130°C fan/gas 2.

Heat the duck fat in a medium-sized roasting tray over medium heat, until melted. Add the thyme, bay leaves and duck, skin side down, ensuring the duck is covered in the fat. If not, add some more duck fat. Cover the tray with foil and cook slowly in the oven for 4–5 hours until the duck is tender. Remove from the oven and allow to cool slightly, then carefully remove the legs from the fat.

Increase the oven temperature to 180°C/160°C fan/gas 4.

Put the cashew nuts on a baking tray and coat them in the vegetable oil. Season with sea salt and toast in the oven for 8–10 minutes until golden.

Put the duck legs on a separate baking tray, skin side up, and roast in the oven (at the same time as you're toasting the cashew nuts) for 15 minutes. If the skin isn't crisp enough, finish it off under the grill.

To make the dressing, whisk all ingredients together in a bowl.

To assemble the salad, mix the shallots, herbs, rocket and chilli together and divide between four bowls. Add the grapefruit chunks and toasted cashew nuts, then drizzle generously with the dressing. Break up the duck leg meat and place it on top of the salads. Top with the cress (if using) and serve.

Serves: 4
Preparation time: 15 minutes, plus 4 hours salting
Cooking time: 4–5 hours for the confit, 15 minutes for the salad

100g cashew nuts
1 tbsp vegetable oil
2 shallots, finely sliced
½ bunch of coriander, leaves picked
½ bunch of mint, leaves picked
100g rocket, finely chopped
1 green chilli, deseeded and finely sliced
1 pink grapefruit, peeled, segmented and cut into 1cm chunks
red amaranth cress, to serve (optional)
sea salt

FOR THE CONFIT DUCK
4 skin-on duck legs
250g rock salt
800g duck fat
¼ bunch of thyme
2 bay leaves

FOR THE DRESSING
3 tbsp rice wine vinegar
100ml sesame oil
1 tbsp runny honey
3cm piece of fresh ginger, peeled and finely grated
1 tsp white miso paste

The combination of the pork, creamy beans and punchy salsa verde is a winning dish. Due to the availability of rare-breed varietals and good pig-farming practices, I do tend to cook my pork on the medium side, so a blush of light pink remains in the centre.

PORK CHOPS WITH SALSA VERDE AND WHITE BEANS

If using dried beans, place the drained and rinsed haricot beans in a medium saucepan with the carrot, celery, garlic and bay leaves and cover with cold water. Bring to the boil, reduce to a gentle simmer and cook for 1 hour–1 hour 15 minutes, or until the beans are soft.

While the beans are cooking, preheat the oven to 200°C/180°C fan/gas 6.

To make the salsa verde, place all the ingredients in a mini food processor and pulse until you have a chunky sauce. Add sea salt to taste and set aside.

Heat the vegetable oil in a griddle pan or frying pan over high heat. Rinse the brined pork chops under cold running water and pat them dry with kitchen paper. When the oil is almost smoking, add the chops and fry them for approximately 3 minutes on each side, in batches if necessary. Place the seared chops on a roasting tray and transfer to the oven to cook for a further 5 minutes. Remove and allow to rest for 5 minutes.

Drain the haricot beans and transfer them to a large bowl. Gently stir through the salsa verde. Serve the chops with the beans and a dollop of crème fraîche.

Serves: 4
Preparation time: 10 minutes, plus 2 hours brining and soaking
Cooking time: 1 hour 15 minutes

180g dried haricot beans, soaked in water overnight, drained and rinsed well (or 1 x 400g tin haricot beans, drained)
1 carrot, halved
1 celery stick, halved
2 garlic bulbs, halved
2 bay leaves
25ml vegetable oil
4 large pork chops (approx. 900g in total), brined (page 77)
sea salt and freshly ground black pepper
4 tbsp crème fraîche, to serve

FOR THE SALSA VERDE
2 heaped tbsp finely chopped tarragon
¼ bunch of flat-leaf parsley, leaves picked
20g capers in brine
grated zest and juice of 1 lemon
125ml extra virgin olive oil

Homemade burgers are a great meal for summer time, or in winter when you need a pick-me-up. I am a big fan of chorizo as it has such a powerful flavour – it is very useful as a seasoning as well as an ingredient in its own right. Here it adds a punch and taste to the standard burger, especially with the spicy mayonnaise.

PORK AND CHORIZO BURGERS

To make the patties, remove the skin from the chorizo and finely dice or crumble the meat (blitz it in a small food processor if you have one to hand). Put it in a bowl and combine with all the remaining patty ingredients. Heat the oil in a large frying pan over a medium-high heat, form a teaspoon-sized patty and fry it until it's cooked through, then check the seasoning, adding more condiments or salt if you like. Shape the mix into 4 patties and place on a plate in the fridge, covered, for at least 2 hours, or until needed (you can make them up to 24 hours ahead of time, if you wish).

Mix the mayonnaise in a bowl with the paprika, sriracha and gherkins. Set aside.

Preheat the oven to 200°C/180°C fan/gas 6. Reheat the oil in the large frying pan over medium-high heat. When hot, add the patties and fry them for 2½–3½ minutes on each side until dark brown, then transfer to a roasting tray. Place in the oven for 10–15 minutes or until the juices run clear, placing a slice of Cheddar cheese on top of each burger for the final 5 minutes.

To serve, halve and toast the buns and spread the mayonnaise on the inside of the top (and bottom) of each one. Sandwich them together with rocket and a patty in each.

Makes: 4 burgers
Preparation time: 20 minutes
Cooking time: 20–25 minutes

2 tbsp vegetable oil
4 slices of Cheddar cheese
50g rocket
4 burger buns

FOR THE MEAT PATTIES
100g cooking chorizo
300g minced pork
1 onion, finely diced
2 tbsp tomato ketchup
1 tbsp Worcestershire sauce
½ tsp sweet smoked paprika
2 tbsp chopped coriander leaves
2 eggs
6 water biscuits, finely crushed
½ tsp table salt

FOR THE SPICED MAYONNAISE
6 tbsp good-quality mayonnaise
1 tsp sweet smoked paprika
2 tsp sriracha sauce (hot chilli sauce)
8 pickled gherkins, finely diced

Pork fillet tends to be less popular than other prime cuts, but it is reasonably priced and very tasty. The Spanish quince paste, membrillo, is a really good ingredient to have in your fridge, not just to enjoy with cheese as it's typically served, but to add to both sweet and savoury dishes, too.

PORK FILLET WITH PINE-NUT CRUMB AND CHARRED CABBAGE

Serves: 4
Preparation time: 15 minutes, plus
    2 hours brining
Cooking time: 45 minutes

600–800g pork fillet, brined (page 77)
sea salt and freshly ground black
    pepper

To make the sauce, heat the vegetable oil in a medium saucepan over medium-high heat. When hot, add the onion and table salt and fry for about 10 minutes, stirring frequently, until the onion turns a deep golden brown. Add the garlic and rosemary and cook for a further 2 minutes, then add the stock and bring to the boil. Reduce the heat and simmer very gently for 30 minutes.

While the sauce is simmering, make the pine-nut crumb. Roughly chop the pine nuts and mix them in a bowl with the rosemary, then season lightly.

Remove the rosemary sprigs from the sauce and whisk in the quince paste, then remove the sauce from the heat, pass it through a fine sieve and whisk in the crème fraîche to finish. Add a little more salt, if you like.

For the cabbage, preheat the oven to 200°C/180°C fan/gas 6 and line a baking tray with foil. Heat the chicken stock in a small saucepan and whisk in the butter, ½ teaspoon of sea salt and a pinch of pepper. Add the thyme. Place the cabbage quarters on the lined tray, ensuring the foil is large enough to encase the cabbage, then pour over the stock and butter emulsion, including the thyme sprigs. Enclose tightly with the foil, so no steam can escape, then bake for 15 minutes.

Meanwhile, heat a griddle pan until smoking. Rinse the pork fillet under cold running water and dry with kitchen paper. Place it on the hot griddle pan and sear it all over, then transfer it to a baking tray and place in the oven for 15–20 minutes, or until the juices run clear. Leave to rest, loosely covered in foil, for 5 minutes.

Chargrill the cabbage on the griddle pan for about 3 minutes on each sliced side.

To serve, brush the pork fillets all over with the sauce then coat them in the crumb. Carve the fillet into four pieces then sit them on a plate with the cabbage. Drizzle with the sauce to finish.

FOR THE QUINCE AND ROSEMARY SAUCE
2 tbsp vegetable oil
1 onion, finely sliced
½ tsp table salt
1 garlic clove, crushed with the side of
    a knife
2 sprigs of rosemary
200ml Chicken or Vegetable Stock
    (pages 83 and 57)
4 tbsp quince paste (membrillo)
2 tbsp crème fraîche

FOR THE PINE-NUT CRUMB
4 tbsp pine nuts, toasted
1 tbsp finely chopped rosemary needles

FOR THE CHARRED CABBAGE
50ml Chicken Stock (page 83)
25g butter
4 sprigs of thyme
1 Hispi (or pointed) cabbage, quartered

This recipe is a take on a classic sausage and mash. Using the traditional Cumberland sausage rings makes for an interesting-looking dish and adds something a little different to a meal, especially if no one knows what is underneath! Green beans or creamed spinach make great accompaniments.

CUMBERLAND SAUSAGE, ONION AND POTATO PIE

Serves: 4
Preparation time: 20 minutes
Cooking time: 1 hour 10 minutes

2 tbsp vegetable oil
1 large ring (or 4 small rings) of good-
    quality Cumberland sausage
    (approx. 800g in total), or
    12 sausages, arranged as a ring
6 tbsp panko breadcrumbs
25g soft butter
30g grated Cheddar cheese
freshly ground black pepper

Preheat the oven to 200°C/180°C fan/gas 6.

To make the onion gravy, heat the oil in a frying pan over medium heat, add the onions and fry for 15–20 minutes, stirring frequently, until soft and golden. Stir in the flour and cook it for a minute or so then gradually add the beef stock, followed by the other ingredients, stirring well. Bring to the boil, then reduce the heat to low and simmer for 15–20 minutes, stirring occasionally. Taste and add more salt if necessary.

While the gravy is simmering, make the mash. Place the potatoes in a pan of salted water and bring to the boil. Simmer for 15–20 minutes, until tender, then drain well, return to the pan off the heat and mash with the melted butter and milk or cream until smooth. Add the table salt and egg yolks and mix well.

Heat the vegetable oil in a large frying pan over medium-high heat. When hot, fry the sausage ring(s) for about 10 minutes, turning it to brown it on all sides. Place in a round baking dish, around 23cm in diameter and cover with the gravy. Spoon or pipe the mash on top to cover completely.

Mix the panko crumbs with the soft butter, grated cheese and a good pinch of black pepper. Sprinkle over the mash.

Bake for 25–30 minutes, until the sausage is cooked through and the potato is golden. Serve hot.

FOR THE ONION GRAVY

2 tbsp vegetable oil
2 onions, thinly sliced
2 tbsp plain flour
300ml Beef Stock (page 137)
2 garlic cloves, finely grated
4 tbsp Worcestershire sauce
1 tbsp picked thyme leaves
pinch of sea salt

FOR THE MASHED POTATO

400g King Edward potatoes (or other
    floury potato), peeled and cut into
    large equal-sized chunks
50g butter, melted
150ml milk or double cream
pinch of table salt
2 egg yolks

Macaroni cheese is one of the best comfort foods. The addition of the bacon jam to my version, however, takes it to the next level. It is a bowl of pure enjoyment, and well worth the extra effort involved.

MACARONI CHEESE WITH BACON JAM

To make the bacon jam, heat the oil in a saucepan over medium-high heat. Add the bacon, onion and garlic, and fry for about 10 minutes, until the bacon is starting to colour and the onion is soft. Add the remaining ingredients, reduce the heat to low and cook, stirring frequently, for 30 minutes.

To make the cheese sauce, melt the butter in a medium saucepan until foaming. Add the flour and whisk well for 30 seconds–1 minute, then gradually whisk in the milk and bring to a very gentle simmer. Cook for about 2 minutes, until thickened. Stir in the cheese, mustard, Worcestershire sauce, season with sea salt and pepper and remove from the heat.

Preheat the oven to 220°C/200°C fan/gas 7.

Cook the macaroni in boiling salted water for 2 minutes less than it says on the packet instructions. Drain and mix with the cheese sauce until the pasta is thoroughly coated. Spoon into 6 individual ovenproof dishes or one large 20 x 20cm dish. Spoon the bacon jam on top, then finish with the grated Gruyère.

Bake in the oven for 15 minutes until bubbling and golden on top.

Serves: 6
Preparation time: 20 minutes
Cooking time: 55 minutes

325g dried macaroni pasta
100g Gruyère cheese, grated
sea salt and freshly ground black
    pepper

FOR THE BACON JAM
2 tbsp vegetable oil
250g smoked streaky bacon, very
    finely chopped
1 onion, finely chopped
1 garlic clove, finely grated
¼ tsp coriander seeds, crushed
1 tsp sweet smoked paprika
1 tbsp sherry vinegar
½ tsp freshly ground black pepper
2 tbsp tomato purée
1 tbsp black treacle

FOR THE CHEESE SAUCE
75g butter
75g plain flour
650ml whole milk
150g grated mature Cheddar cheese
1 tsp Dijon mustard
1 tsp Worcestershire sauce

Pork belly is a joint that needs to be cooked at a gentle heat, for quite some time, to ensure it is tender as the heat breaks down the sinew. Cooking it over a long time also helps render off some of the fat, making the meat less rich and the crackling crispier. The burnt pear adds a smoky sweetness to this dish that really enhances the flavour.

SLOW-COOKED PORK BELLY WITH BURNT PEAR AND NUTMEG

Score the skin of the pork belly with shallow cuts 5mm apart (make sure you don't cut right through to the flesh – about 3mm depth is ideal). Grate half the nutmeg into a bowl, add the rock salt, 6 sprigs of the thyme and the sugar, mix to combine, then rub it over the pork belly skin. Cover and chill in the fridge for at least 12 hours (up to 24 hours). Thoroughly rinse the salt mix off the pork under cold running water then pat dry with kitchen paper.

Preheat the oven to 150°C/130°C fan/gas 2.

Put the onions, finely sliced pears, remaining thyme sprigs, cloves and the chicken stock in a large roasting dish and grate in the remaining nutmeg. Place the pork belly on top, skin side up, cover with foil and place in the oven for 3 hours. For the last hour, brush the 2 whole peeled pears with the maple syrup or honey, place them in a small ovenproof dish and put them in the oven too.

Remove the pork roasting dish and the pears from the oven. Gently place the pork on a baking tray. Remove the thyme sprigs and cloves and discard, then blitz everything else in a blender, including the cooking juices. Keep warm.

Turn your oven to medium grill setting (or preheat your separate grill to medium). Put the pork belly back in the roasting tray and put the tray on a shelf about 15cm away from the grill. Place the roasted pears on the shelf, too, and grill slowly until the crackling crisps up – this should take 15–20 minutes.

When the belly has crisped up, remove it from the grill and loosely cover it with foil. Remove the baked pears, carefully cut them in half lengthways. Place them directly under the grill cut side up, until they begin to blacken, then remove. Carve the rested pork belly and serve it with the pear and onion sauce and the burnt pears.

Serves: 4
Preparation time: 15 minutes, plus minimum 12 hours marinating
Cooking time: 3 hours 25 minutes

1 piece of boneless pork belly (550–650g)
1 nutmeg
50g rock salt
10 sprigs of thyme
2 tbsp demerara sugar
2 onions, finely sliced
4 pears, peeled, 2 of them halved, cored and finely sliced
4 cloves
200ml Chicken Stock (page 83)
1 tbsp maple syrup or runny honey

Surf and turf – combining meat with seafood – is quite common in a lot of Asian and American cuisines, and it works so well. Prawns with shells on are generally only available from a fishmonger, but do try to source them, as the shells enhance the flavour of the broth considerably. You can use the prawns, once they're shelled, for the Prawn, Sugar Snap, Kale, Peanut and Coriander Salad on page 151.

SPICED PORK AND PRAWN BROTH WITH SLOW-COOKED PORK BELLY

Score the skin of the pork belly with shallow cuts 5mm apart (make sure you don't cut right through to the flesh – about 3mm depth is ideal), and place the belly on a plate. Mix the rock salt, thyme and sugar together and coat the skin of the pork belly in the mixture. Cover and chill in the fridge for at least 12 hours (up to 24 hours). Thoroughly rinse the salt mix off the pork under cold running water then pat the pork dry with kitchen paper.

Preheat the oven to 190°C/170°C fan/gas 5.

Put the pork spare ribs in a roasting tray and place in the oven for 30–35 minutes, until a light golden colour. Remove from the oven, add the shallots and garlic, then return to the oven and cook for a further 10 minutes.

Heat the vegetable oil in a large saucepan over medium-high heat. When almost smoking, add the prawn shells and brown them well – they will turn a deep red colour. Add the chilli and dried shrimp and cook for a further 3–4 minutes. Add the roasted ribs, shallots and garlic, being sure to scrape all of the cooking residue from the roasting tray into the saucepan. Add the star anise, chicken stock, 1 litre of water, lemongrass and coriander stalks and bring to a simmer.

Simmer for 1 hour then strain the liquid through a sieve into a large saucepan. Discard the prawn shells and vegetables. Using a fork, scrape the meat off the spare ribs into the liquid. Add the pork belly to the liquid, place the pan over very low heat, cover and simmer for 3 hours, or until a knife inserted into the pork belly meets no resistance. Remove the pork belly and place it on a baking tray skin side up.

Serves: 6
Preparation time: 20 minutes
    (if you are shelling the prawns),
    plus minimum 12 hours marinating
Cooking time: 5 hours and 20 minutes

1 piece of boneless pork belly
    (550–650g)
50g rock salt
6 sprigs of thyme
2 tbsp demerara sugar
500g pork spare ribs
4 shallots, finely sliced
1 garlic bulb, halved horizontally
4 tbsp vegetable oil
prawn shells from 250g raw prawns
1 red chilli, deseeded and thinly sliced
30g dried shrimp
3 star anise
1 litre Chicken Stock (page 83)
2 lemongrass stalks, bashed
1 bunch of coriander, leaves and stalks
    separated
150g vermicelli noodles
½ bunch of mint, leaves finely chopped
lime wedges, to serve

Heat your grill to a medium setting (or if you only have a high setting, place the rack halfway down the oven). Grill the pork belly for 10–15 minutes until the skin is crispy, keeping a close eye on it so that it doesn't burn.

Remove the pork belly from the grill, leave it to cool slightly then slice it into 1cm-thick strips.

Cook the vermicelli noodles according to the packet instructions, then add them to the broth.

Ladle the broth into bowls, top with the pork belly and serve with the coriander leaves, chopped mint and lime wedges.

This is one of my favourite dishes. The meat literally falls off the bone and it's absolutely delicious. Smoking food at home can be a little daunting at first, so try it on a warm day when you can open all the windows! No cutlery is needed here!

SMOKY PORK RIBS WITH BOURBON AND APPLE GLAZE

Heat a dry frying pan over medium heat, add the cumin, coriander, fennel, onion and yellow mustard seeds and toast them for 4–6 minutes until fragrant. Transfer them to a spice grinder or pestle and mortar and crush until they form a powder. Mix the powder with the other spice rub ingredients and coat the racks of ribs with the rub. Wrap them in clingfilm and chill for 12 hours.

To make the glaze, pour the apple juice into a saucepan over medium heat. Bring to the boil and let it rapidly simmer and reduce by two-thirds until you have 100ml of juice left. Add the bourbon and simmer for 2 minutes, then remove from the heat and set aside.

If you have a barbecue with a lid, heat it to a low heat, unwrap the ribs and place them on the rack for 4 hours with the lid closed, taking care that the temperature stays around 110°C. If you are using an oven, preheat it to 130°C/110°C fan/gas ¾ and place the ribs directly on the oven racks, with a tray at the bottom of the oven to catch drips. Cook for 4 hours then remove from the oven. To finish, turn on the grill setting on your oven. When hot, grill the racks on both sides until golden and sizzling. Keep a close eye on them, as this will only take a matter of minutes. Gently reheat the glaze, as it will have set as it cooled due to the pectin in the apple juice, then brush it liberally over the ribs and serve immediately.

Serves: 4–6 (4 generously)
Preparation time: 10 minutes, plus
    12 hours marinating
Cooking time: 4 hours 5 minutes

4 x 500–600g racks of pork back ribs

FOR THE SPICE RUB
1 tsp cumin seeds
1 tsp coriander seeds
½ tsp fennel seeds
1 tsp onion seeds
2 tsp yellow mustard seeds
40g table salt
50g caster sugar
50g soft dark brown sugar
10g smoked sweet paprika
10g English mustard powder
5g chilli powder

FOR THE GLAZE
300ml cloudy apple juice
25ml bourbon

'Nduja is a spreadable, spicy, chorizo-like meat spread from Italy. It has many uses – try it in seafood pasta – adding both flavour and heat to any dish, and has a good shelf life, making it a great fridge staple. You can buy it fresh from most supermarket deli sections, or in a jar. Fresh 'nduja is preferable but the flavour can still be very good from the jarred product.

PORK SCHNITZEL WITH 'NDUJA AIOLI

Preheat the oven to 200°C/180°C fan/gas 6.

To make the aioli, slice the top off the garlic bulb, sit it in a piece of foil and rub it with a little olive oil and some sea salt. Wrap the foil around the garlic and roast it in the oven for 45 minutes.

Unwrap the garlic, and when cool enough, squeeze the flesh into a bowl. Mash with a fork until completely smooth. Cover and leave to cool completely.

Put the egg yolks in a bowl and, using a balloon whisk, mix in the vinegar and Dijon mustard. Put the vegetable oil and the 175ml of olive oil in a jug and slowly drizzle them into the egg yolk mixture, whisking continuously. When the mixture has a mayonnaise consistency, whisk in the 'nduja until well combined. Stir in the garlic purée and lemon juice and zest and season with sea salt. If not using straight away, store it in the fridge, covered, for up to 3 days.

Place the pork loin steaks between two sheets of clingfilm or baking parchment. Pound them flat with a rolling pin until 6mm thick.

Put the flour for the crumb in a wide, shallow bowl and season it with black pepper. Put the beaten eggs in a separate shallow bowl and the breadcrumbs in a third shallow bowl. Rinse the brined pork under cold running water and pat dry with kitchen paper, then coat each piece in the seasoned flour, followed by the beaten egg and finish them with a generous coating of breadcrumbs. Place on a plate and chill in the fridge for 10 minutes.

Pour enough vegetable oil into a large non-stick frying pan to come up to about 1cm and place over medium/medium-high heat. Fry the schnitzels, two at a time, for around 4 minutes per side, using a metal spoon to baste them frequently with the hot oil, until they are crispy and cooked through. Lift out with a fish slice, drain and serve with the 'nduja aioli and wedges of lemon.

Serves: 4
Preparation time: 20 minutes, plus
    10 minutes chilling and
    2 hours brining
Cooking time: around 1 hour
    10 minutes

4 thin pork loin steaks or escalopes,
    brined (page 77)
vegetable oil, for shallow-frying
lemon wedges, to serve

FOR THE SCHNITZEL CRUMB
50g plain flour
2 eggs, beaten
150g panko breadcrumbs (or dried
    breadcrumbs)
freshly ground black pepper

FOR THE 'NDUJA AIOLI
1 garlic bulb
175ml olive oil, plus extra to rub the
    garlic
3 egg yolks
1 tbsp white wine vinegar
½ tsp Dijon mustard
50ml vegetable oil
40g 'nduja
grated zest and juice of 1 lemon
sea salt

I first tried something similar to this in Mauritius, which was a lamb curry with banana. I wanted to recreate it on a more simple level, so I came up with these koftas. Lamb generally has a high fat content, and that is where all of the flavour is, so use a slightly fattier mince to get the maximum flavour. I like to eat this with naan bread and green salad.

SPICED LAMB KOFTA WITH BANANA CHUTNEY

Serves: 4
Preparation time: 20 minutes
Cooking time: 20 minutes

To make the koftas, heat a small dry frying pan over medium heat, add the cumin seeds and toast them until fragrant. Tip them into a pestle and mortar or spice grinder and crush them to a powder. Mix the crushed seeds in a bowl with all the other ingredients for the koftas, except the mince and oil, then add the lamb and mix well. Shape the mixture into eight sausages.

Preheat the oven to 200°C/180°C fan/gas 6 and line a baking tray with foil.

Heat the vegetable oil in a large frying pan over medium heat. When hot, add four of the koftas and fry them for 7–10 minutes until golden all over. Repeat with the remaining four koftas. Place all the koftas on the lined tray and transfer to the oven for a further 7–10 minutes, until cooked through.

To make the banana chutney, put all the ingredients in a blender or food processor and blend until smooth. Adjust seasoning if necessary.

Serve the koftas, while hot, with the chutney and either steamed white rice or naan bread and salad.

FOR THE KOFTA
1 tbsp cumin seeds
1 onion, finely diced
½ tsp ground turmeric
½ tsp ground coriander
1 green chilli, deseeded and finely diced
2 garlic cloves, grated
2 tbsp chopped mint leaves
2 tbsp chopped flat-leaf parsley
2 tbsp chopped coriander
50g pistachio nuts, chopped
½ tbsp table salt
2 tbsp soy sauce
1 egg, beaten
500g minced lamb
2 tbsp vegetable oil

FOR THE BANANA CHUTNEY
1 ripe banana, mashed
1 green chilli, deseeded and finely diced
grated zest and juice of 1 lime
2 tbsp ground coriander
2 tbsp chopped mint leaves
2 tbsp Greek yoghurt
½ tsp sea salt
½ tsp ground turmeric

I came up with this recipe when I was working on my skills test for *MasterChef: The Professionals*. It was such a hit with the viewers that I thought it vital I included it in this book. It reminds me of a roast lamb dinner, with peas and fresh mint, and malt vinegar, all in a baguette.

WARM LAMB NECK AND MINTED PEA BAGUETTE

Season the lamb neck slices with sea salt and pepper then coat them in the flour. Shake off the excess flour.

Heat 2 tablespoons of the vegetable oil in a large frying pan. When smoking, add the herbs then add half the lamb slices and brown them for 1½ minutes on each side. Transfer to a dish then brown the remaining lamb slices (cooking them in batches avoids overcrowding the pan). Cover the browned lamb with foil and leave in a warm place to rest. Deglaze the pan with 2 tablespoons of the malt vinegar and simmer for 1 minute. Reduce the heat to medium-low, add the beef stock and the teaspoon of mustard and cook for 4 minutes. Pour the sauce over the lamb neck slices and re-cover with the foil.

Heat the remaining 2 tablespoons of vegetable oil in a medium frying pan over medium heat. When warm, add the shallots and a pinch of sea salt and cook gently for about 7 minutes, until soft and translucent. Add the remaining malt vinegar and cook for a further 5 minutes, until syrupy. Add the rest of the mustard, stir well, then add the peas. When warmed through, add the mint.

Brush the olive oil on the inside of the baguette and rub with the garlic clove. Lay the lamb slices on the base of 4 of the baguette slices. Pour over the sauce. Add the pea mix, and scatter with mint leaves, then finish with the baguette top. Serve warm.

Serves: 4

Preparation time: 10 minutes

Cooking time: around 25 minutes

2 lamb neck fillets (150–200g each), cut into 1cm-thick slices

4 tbsp plain flour

4 tbsp vegetable oil

2 sprigs of rosemary

2 sprigs of thyme

6 tbsp malt vinegar

100ml Beef Stock (page 137)

1 tsp Dijon mustard, plus 1 tbsp

2 shallots, finely diced

150g frozen peas, defrosted and crushed with a fork

2 tbsp chopped mint, plus leaves to serve

2 tbsp olive oil

1 baguette, cut into 4, then cut in half horizontally

1 garlic clove, peeled

sea salt and freshly ground black pepper

The combination of flavours in this recipe works wonderfully, with a kick of spice complemented by the fresh mint and cool yoghurt. If you are not a fan of spice, just leave out the harissa and marinate the lamb in olive oil.

HARISSA-MARINATED LAMB WITH MINT CHUTNEY, PISTACHIOS AND YOGHURT DRESSING

Mix 2 teaspoons of the harissa paste with the olive oil. Rinse the brined lamb rumps under cold running water and pat them dry with kitchen paper. Rub the harissa mix over the lamb rumps, place them in a container and chill for at least 6 hours (up to 12 hours).

Preheat the oven to 200°C/180°C fan/gas 6.

To make the fresh mint chutney, heat the malt vinegar in a small saucepan. Add the sugar and dissolve over medium heat. Remove the pan from the heat and add the shallots. When cool, add the oil and set aside until ready to use.

To make the yoghurt dressing, mix all ingredients together in a bowl with the last teaspoon of harissa paste and season to taste.

Heat the vegetable oil in a large frying pan over medium heat. When hot, place the lamb rumps, fat side down, in the pan. Cook for 5–8 minutes, until the fat begins to render and turn a lovely golden brown. Turn the rumps over and seal on all the other sides for a further 5 minutes, then place them on a foil-lined dish in the oven. Bake for 5–10 minutes, depending on how pink you like your lamb. Remove from the oven, cover with foil and leave somewhere warm to rest for 5 minutes.

Finish the mint chutney by adding the chopped fresh mint. Serve the lamb rumps with the mint chutney and yoghurt dressing, sprinkled with the pistachio nuts. Serve with a large green salad or roasted vegetables.

Serves: 4
Preparation time: 20 minutes, plus 2 hours brining and 6–12 hours marinating
Cooking time: 25 minutes

3 tsp harissa paste
4 tbsp olive oil
4 lamb rumps (180–220g each), brined (page 77)
2 tbsp vegetable oil
30g pistachio nuts, toasted and roughly chopped

FOR THE FRESH MINT CHUTNEY
6 tbsp malt vinegar
2 tsp caster sugar
4 shallots, finely sliced
4 tbsp olive oil
1 bunch of mint, leaves separated and finely chopped

FOR THE YOGHURT DRESSING
150g Greek yoghurt
¼ cucumber, grated (around 150g)
1 tsp cumin seeds, toasted and crushed
sea salt

Asparagus is one of my favourite spring ingredients. The fact it is in season for such a fleeting time adds to its wonder and appeal. The classic pairing of asparagus with lamb is enhanced here by the addition of a rich and creamy Parmesan sauce. To ensure your asparagus spears do not have tough ends, just snap them at the base to remove.

LAMB CHOPS WITH ASPARAGUS, PARMESAN SAUCE AND MARJORAM

Bring a large pan of salted water to the boil. Blanch the asparagus for 2 minutes then drain and cool under cold running water to stop it cooking any further.

Heat a griddle pan over high heat until very hot. Brush the lamb chops all over with a little olive oil and season with sea salt and pepper on both sides. Sit the chops fat-side down on the griddle, leaning them up against each other for support. Cook for 4–5 minutes until the fat renders and becomes crisp.

Lay the chops flat on their sides and cook for a further 3–5 minutes on each side, basting them with the rendered fat. Remove the chops from the pan and set aside to rest for 5 minutes.

While the lamb chops are cooking, make the Parmesan sauce. Heat the chicken stock in a large frying pan over high heat. Bring to the boil and let it bubble until it has reduced by half. Whisk in the Parmesan cheese, crème fraîche, lemon zest and juice and add a couple of twists of black pepper. When the Parmesan has melted, add the asparagus to the pan and heat through. Finish with the marjoram and serve with the lamb chops.

Serves: 4
Preparation time: 10 minutes
Cooking time: 15 minutes

2 bunches of asparagus (about 500g), tough ends trimmed and sliced in half diagonally
8 lamb loin chops
olive oil, for brushing
½ bunch of marjoram, leaves picked (or sage or oregano)
sea salt and freshly ground black pepper

FOR THE PARMESAN SAUCE
200ml Chicken Stock (page 83)
25g finely grated Parmesan cheese
2 tbsp crème fraîche
finely grated zest and juice of ½ lemon

Lamb stew with dumplings is a winning winter dish and the tarragon adds the perfect top note of flavour. We use tarragon a lot in the restaurant kitchens and I would always recommend having a bunch in your fridge at home. The stew can be made a couple of days before you serve it to let the flavours really develop, then just finish off with the dumplings before you eat.

LAMB STEW WITH TARRAGON DUMPLINGS

Serves: 4
Preparation time: 30 minutes
Cooking time: around 3 hours

Heat the oil in a large casserole dish over medium-high heat. Coat the lamb in the flour and table salt and brown well in the oil for 5–7 minutes, in batches, adding more oil if necessary. Remove, and set aside.

Preheat the oven to 160°C/140°C fan/gas 3.

Add the onions and cumin seeds to the casserole dish. Season with sea salt and lightly caramelise the onions, stirring, for about 10 minutes. Add the tomato purée, red wine and herbs and simmer until the red wine has reduced to a syrup. Add the stock and simmer for a further 5 minutes. Remove the bay leaves, rosemary and thyme from the stew and discard. Add the lamb back to the dish, cover, and bake in the oven for 2 hours.

About 30 minutes before the lamb is ready, make the dumplings. Rub the butter into the flour with the tarragon, baking powder and table salt. Add enough milk to the mix to make a firm dough. Roll the dough into eight balls and chill for 20 minutes.

Remove the lamb stew from the oven and increase the oven temperature to 200°C/180°C fan/gas 6.

Add the diced carrot, parsnip and sweet potato to the lamb stew and simmer on the hob for 5 minutes.

Top with the dumplings, cover the dish loosely with greased foil, and place back in the oven for 15 minutes. Remove the foil and bake for a further 10 minutes, until the dumplings have risen and a skewer inserted into a dumpling comes out clean, then serve.

2 tbsp vegetable oil, plus extra if needed
600g braising lamb (neck or shoulder), diced
3 tbsp plain flour
½ tsp table salt
2 onions, diced
1 tsp cumin seeds, lightly crushed
2 tbsp tomato purée
250ml red wine
2 bay leaves
½ bunch of rosemary
½ bunch of thyme
600ml lamb stock
sea salt
1 carrot, cut into 5mm–1cm dice
1 small parsnip, cut into 5mm–1cm dice
1 small sweet potato (about 200g), peeled and cut into 5mm–1cm dice

FOR THE TARRAGON DUMPLINGS
50g cold butter, diced
90g plain flour
1 tbsp finely chopped tarragon
1 tsp baking powder
¼ tsp table salt
50–60ml milk

Polenta is a great storecupboard ingredient. It cooks quickly and works as an accompaniment to almost any meat, fish or vegetable dish. I always use yellow quick-cook polenta, as it absorbs liquid faster than the coarser variety. We always have a packet in the cupboard as a 'go to' for a quick supper.

LAMB RUMP WITH POLENTA AND ARTICHOKE SALAD

Preheat the oven to 200°C/180°C fan/gas 6 and line a baking dish with foil.

To make the artichoke salad, mix all ingredients together in a bowl. Cover with clingfilm and set aside until ready to serve.

Heat the vegetable oil in a large frying pan over medium heat. Rinse the brined lamb rumps under cold running water and pat them dry with kitchen paper. When the oil's hot, place the lamb rumps, fat side down, in the pan. Cook for about 7 minutes, until the fat begins to render and turn a lovely golden brown, then turn the rumps over and seal the other side. Transfer to the foil-lined dish and bake in the oven for 5–10 minutes, depending on how pink you like your lamb. Remove from the oven, cover with foil and leave somewhere warm to rest for 5 minutes.

To make the polenta, place the milk, stock, butter and saffron (if using) in a medium saucepan over high heat. Bring to the boil, then whisk in the polenta. Reduce the heat and keep stirring for a few minutes until the polenta no longer tastes grainy. Add the Parmesan and mix well. Season to taste.

Place a generous spoonful of the polenta in four deep bowls. Carve the rested lamb rumps and place on top. Finish with the artichoke salad, and serve.

Serves: 4
Preparation time: 20 minutes, plus 2 hours brining
Cooking time: 15 minutes

2 tbsp vegetable oil
4 lamb rumps (180–220g each), brined (page 77)

FOR THE ARTICHOKE SALAD
6 globe artichokes from a tin or jar, drained and quartered
100g semi-dried tomatoes, finely chopped
1 tbsp capers in brine, strained and finely chopped
2 tbsp finely chopped tarragon
2 tbsp extra virgin olive oil
1 tbsp white wine vinegar

FOR THE POLENTA
250ml milk
125ml Chicken or Vegetable Stock (page 83 and 57)
60g butter
pinch of saffron (optional)
60g yellow quick-cook polenta
30g grated Parmesan cheese
sea salt

Lamb shanks are such a flavoursome joint of meat. Slow-cooked in a sauce with simple flavours, they are a perfect winter supper, especially here with the warmth of saffron, cumin, fennel seeds and coriander seeds. They also work superbly in a slow cooker, if you happen to have one.

SAFFRON-BRAISED LAMB SHANKS

Preheat the oven to 160°C/140°C fan/gas 3.

Heat 2 tablespoons of the vegetable oil in a large casserole dish over medium-high heat. Rinse the brined lamb shanks under cold running water and pat them dry with kitchen paper. When the oil's hot, dust the shanks with the flour then add them to the hot oil and brown them all over, two at a time, for 7–10 minutes. Once browned, remove from the casserole dish and set aside.

Add the remaining 2 tablespoons of vegetable oil to the same casserole dish, and when hot, add the onion, carrots, celery, garlic, spices, rosemary and bay leaves. Cook over medium-high heat for 10–15 minutes, stirring, until the vegetables are a deep golden colour. Add the tomato purée, stir well, then deglaze the pan with the white wine and sherry. Simmer rapidly for 7 minutes, then add the stock and saffron and simmer for a further 10 minutes.

Add the browned lamb shanks to the casserole dish and cover with a lid. Place in the oven for 2½–3 hours, or until a knife inserted into the shanks meets no resistance. Carefully remove the shanks from the pan, transfer to a serving plate and cover to keep warm. Strain the sauce into a large saucepan, bring to a simmer and reduce to your desired consistency, then season to taste. Spoon the sauce over the shanks and serve.

Serves: 4
Preparation time: 20 minutes, plus
    2 hours brining
Cooking time: about 3 hours
    45 minutes

4 tbsp vegetable oil
4 lamb shanks, brined (page 77)
3 tbsp plain flour
1 large onion, quartered
2 carrots, quartered
2 celery sticks, quartered
4 garlic cloves, peeled and left whole
½ tsp cumin seeds
½ tsp fennel seeds
½ tsp coriander seeds
½ bunch of rosemary
3 bay leaves
4 tbsp tomato purée
250ml white wine
4 tbsp sweet sherry
500ml lamb or Beef Stock (page 137)
good pinch of saffron strands
sea salt and freshly ground black
    pepper

Roast leg of lamb is a wonderful British classic, which I have enhanced here by taking a few of the traditional roast accompaniments away and instead created a vibrant and fresh salsa made with herbs, green olives, capers and the salty hit of anchovies. The preserved lemons also add a twist to the classic, taking inspiration from Moroccan dishes of lamb and lemons.

SLOW-COOKED LEG OF LAMB WITH GREEN OLIVE SALSA AND SPICED LEMON

Serves: 4–6
Preparation time: 15 minutes
Cooking time: 2 hours 30 minutes

Preheat the oven to 160°C/140°C fan/gas 3.

Gently score the skin of the lamb with criss-cross marks to create a diamond pattern.

Put the garlic, onions and rosemary in a deep roasting tray. Place the lamb leg on top and sprinkle it generously with freshly ground black pepper. Place in the oven to roast for 2½ hours.

Meanwhile, make the spiced lemon. Put all the ingredients in a saucepan and just cover with water. Bring to the boil then turn down to a simmer and cook gently for 20 minutes. Remove and set aside.

To make the salsa, mix all the ingredients together in a bowl and season to taste with sea salt.

Remove the lamb leg from the oven, cover with foil and allow to rest for 15 minutes, then carve and serve with the salsa and spiced lemon.

1 leg of lamb, bone in, approx. 1.8kg, brined (page 77)
2 garlic bulbs, halved horizontally
2 onions, cut into 2cm-thick slices
1 bunch of rosemary
freshly ground black pepper

FOR THE SPICED LEMON
1 lemon, thinly sliced (as many seeds removed as possible)
½ tsp table salt
1 tsp caster sugar
1 tsp cumin seeds
1 sprig of rosemary

FOR THE OLIVE AND HERB SALSA
½ bunch of mint, finely chopped
1 bunch of flat-leaf parsley, finely chopped
100g Nocellara olives, finely chopped
200ml olive oil
2 tbsp malt vinegar
2 tbsp capers, finely chopped
50g anchovies in oil, finely chopped
sea salt

Mix up your pizza-making with this recipe! I really like the combination of sweet things with blue cheese, hence the honey on this pizza. If you are a little sceptical, leave it off and drizzle a little on a small slice to try. It is the same principle as salted caramel – salty and sweet – and it works very well.

BRESAOLA, BLUE CHEESE AND HONEY PIZZA

To make the pizza dough, put the flour, yeast, sugar and table salt in a large bowl, make a well in the centre and pour in 2 tablespoons of the olive oil with 175ml of warm water. Mix together until you have a wet dough, then turn it out onto a lightly floured work surface and knead for 7–10 minutes until soft and smooth. Alternatively, make the dough in a standmixer fitted with a dough hook.

Transfer the dough to a clean, lightly oiled bowl, cover the bowl with lightly oiled clingfilm and leave to rest in a warm place for about 1 hour, or until the dough has doubled in size.

Tip the risen dough out onto a floured work surface and divide it into two balls. Roll out each ball of dough to a thickness of 5mm and place each pizza base on two well-floured baking sheets.

Spread the cream cheese over both the doughs then scatter them with the sliced onion and a generous amount of freshly ground black pepper. Cover the pizzas loosely with clingfilm and leave to rest for 20 minutes.

Preheat the oven to 220°C/200°C fan/gas 7, grease two more baking sheets each with 1 tablespoon of olive oil and place them in the oven after the pizza bases have been resting for 15 minutes. Let them heat up for 10 minutes.

When ready, carefully remove the hot trays from the oven and slide the pizzas on to them. Bake for 10–12 minutes then place the bresaola on top and bake for a further 5 minutes. Lastly, dot the blue cheese on top, sprinkle the thyme leaves on the pizzas then drizzle with the honey. Bake for a further 3–4 minutes then serve.

Makes: 2 pizzas (serves 2–4)
Preparation time: 30 minutes,
    plus 1 hour 20 minutes rising
    and proving
Cooking time: 20 minutes

8 tbsp cream cheese
1 red onion, finely sliced
80g sliced bresaola
100g soft blue cheese
1 tsp thyme leaves
4 tbsp runny honey
freshly ground black pepper

FOR THE DOUGH
350g strong white bread flour, plus
    extra for dusting
7g sachet fast-action dried yeast or
    easy-bake yeast
1 tsp sugar
½ tsp table salt
4 tbsp olive oil, plus extra for greasing
    and drizzling

Beef Bourguignon is a classic French comfort dish. I have put my own twist on it, with the addition of fennel and new potatoes. The new potatoes braise in the cooking liquor, taking on a wonderful flavour. Try making your own beef stock for an even more savoury plateful. This is a dish you can also make a day or two in advance. I like to serve it with crusty bread and a good bottle of red wine!

BEEF BOURGUIGNON

Preheat the oven to 160°C/140°C fan/gas 3.

Heat 2 tablespoons of the vegetable oil in a large, ovenproof casserole dish over high heat. Mix the flour, table salt and a few twists of pepper together, then toss the steak in the flour and shake off any excess. When the oil is hot, add a batch of the steak and fry until well browned. Remove the steak and set it aside, brown the remaining beef, then remove it and set it aside with the rest.

Add 2 tablespoons of vegetable oil to the casserole over medium-high heat, add the sliced onions and fry for 7–10 minutes, stirring frequently, until soft and golden. Add the garlic, thyme and bay leaves and cook for a further 3 minutes. Add the wine and port and bring to a simmer, scraping the bottom of the dish with a wooden spoon to maximise flavour. After about 10 minutes the alcohol should have reduced to a syrup. At this point, add the beef stock and simmer over medium heat for 20 minutes. Return the beef to the pan, stir well, then cover and place in the oven for 1½ hours.

Remove the casserole from the oven and add the new potatoes. Cover and place back in the oven for a further 1½ hours.

Towards the last 30 minutes of cooking, heat the remaining 2 tablespoons of vegetable oil in a large frying pan over high heat. When hot, add the mushrooms, season well with sea salt and pepper and cook for about 10 minutes until golden and all of the moisture has evaporated. Remove the mushrooms from the pan and set aside. Add the bacon pieces to the hot pan with the fennel. After 5 minutes, add the shallots, reduce the heat and cook the shallots until soft but not browned.

Serves: 4
Preparation time: 25 minutes
Cooking time: around 4 hours

6 tbsp vegetable oil
4 tbsp plain flour
1 tsp table salt
600g braising steak, cut into 2cm chunks
2 onions, thinly sliced
2 garlic cloves, finely grated
½ bunch of thyme, tied together with string
2 bay leaves
300ml red wine
100ml ruby port
600ml Beef Stock (page 137)
400g small new potatoes, scrubbed
200g chestnut mushrooms, quartered
200g smoked back bacon, cut into 1cm chunks
½ fennel bulb, cut into 1cm dice
4 shallots, finely sliced
4 tbsp chopped tarragon
sea salt and freshly ground black pepper

Remove the casserole from the oven. Remove the thyme and bay leaves and gently stir through the mushrooms, bacon, shallots and tarragon. Cover and place back in the oven for 15 minutes. Remove from the oven and leave to rest for 10 minutes before serving.

BEEF STOCK

Heat the oven to 220°C/200°C fan/gas 7. Put the beef bones in a couple of roasting trays and roast for about 30 minutes until dark golden, turning them every so often.

Meanwhile, heat the oil in a large stock pot. Add the carrots, onions, garlic and celery. Cook over high heat until dark golden, then stir in the thyme, bay leaf and tomato purée. Cook for a few minutes.

Lift the roasted bones from the tray and drain off the excess fat. Add the bones to the stock pot. Add 4 litres of cold water and bring to the boil. Skim any discoloured foam/scum from the surface and reduce the heat to low. Simmer for 4–6 hours, skimming occasionally.

Strain the stock through a colander and then through a fine sieve into a clean pan. Bring to the boil and reduce to approximately 1.5 litres.

Use straight away or cool and chill in the fridge, using within 3–4 days. Remove any surface fat before using. Alternatively, freeze and use within 4 months.

Makes: approx. 1.5 litres
Preparation time: 10 minutes
Cooking time: 4½–6½ hours

3kg beef bones
3 tbsp vegetable oil
3 carrots, halved
4 onions, quartered
½ garlic bulb
3 celery sticks, halved
½ bunch of thyme
1 bay leaf
3 tbsp tomato purée

Meatballs are another favourite in my household, especially when paired with mozzarella. These meatballs are also jam-packed with herbs, enhancing the flavour of the dish. You can swap the beef mince for pork mince or turkey mince, if you prefer.

HERB AND MOZZARELLA MEATBALL BAKE

Serves: 4–6
Preparation time: 25 minutes
Cooking time: around 1 hour and
    5 minutes

2 x 125g balls buffalo mozzarella,
    drained well, each cut into 8 pieces
½ bunch of basil, leaves chopped
100g Cheddar cheese, grated

FOR THE MEATBALLS
600g minced beef
1 onion, finely diced
4 tbsp tomato ketchup
2 tbsp Worcestershire sauce
2 tbsp finely chopped flat-leaf parsley
    leaves
2 tbsp finely chopped tarragon leaves
2 tbsp finely chopped basil leaves
50g dried breadcrumbs
½ tsp table salt
1 egg, beaten

FOR THE TOMATO SAUCE
6 tbsp vegetable oil
2 onions, finely diced
1 tsp table salt
8 tbsp tomato purée
2 x 400g tins chopped tomatoes
800ml Beef Stock (page 137)
8 tbsp tomato ketchup
8 tbsp Worcestershire sauce
4 bay leaves
2 tsp Dijon mustard

Preheat the oven to 200°C/180°C fan/gas 6.

To make the meatballs, combine all ingredients in a bowl. Divide the mix into 16 and wrap the mince around each piece of mozzarella, to form the meatballs. Cover and chill in the fridge.

To make the tomato sauce, heat 3 tablespoons of the vegetable oil in a medium saucepan over medium-high heat. Add the onions and table salt and cook for 7–10 minutes until soft, then add the tomato purée. Cook for a further 4 minutes then add the remaining ingredients for the sauce. Simmer gently for 25 minutes, stirring regularly, until thick and flavoursome. Remove the bay leaves and blend with a stick blender until smooth. Adjust seasoning if necessary.

Heat the remaining 3 tablespoons of vegetable oil in a large frying pan over medium-high heat. When hot, add the meatballs and brown them for 5 minutes (in batches, so you don't overcrowd the pan). Place the meatballs in a 20cm square baking dish that fits all the meatballs snugly. Cover with the tomato sauce (you might have some left over; if so, freeze it and serve it over pasta) and chopped basil and grated cheese and bake for 20 minutes until bubbling.

The smoky spiciness of chorizo works so well with the beef and the puff pastry that it lifts this traditional dish to a new level. Any braising steak can be used for this recipe, too: cuts with a higher fat content will create a richer base to the pie.

BEEF AND ALE PIE WITH CHORIZO

Preheat the oven to 160°C/140°C fan/gas 3.

Heat 2 tablespoons of the vegetable oil in a large, ovenproof casserole dish over high heat. Mix the flour, 1 teaspoon of the salt and a pinch of black pepper together, then toss the steak in the flour and shake off any excess. When the oil is hot, add a batch of the steak and fry until well browned. Remove the steak and set it aside, brown the remaining beef, then remove it and set it aside with the rest.

Add the remaining 2 tablespoons of vegetable oil to the casserole over medium-high heat, add the shallots and remaining ½ teaspoon of the salt and fry until golden, then add the tomato purée, garlic, thyme and bay leaves and cook for a further 3 minutes. Add the chorizo and cook for a further 3 minutes. Add the ale to the pan and bring to a simmer, scraping the bottom of the dish with a wooden spoon to maximise flavour. When the alcohol has reduced to a syrup, add the beef stock and paprika. Simmer over medium-high heat for 15 minutes to reduce the liquid then return the beef to the pan. Stir well, cover and place in the oven for 2 hours.

Meanwhile, roll out the puff pastry to fit a pie dish around 24cm in diameter, with a 1cm overhang. Place back in the fridge on a baking sheet for 30 minutes to rest.

Remove the casserole from the oven and increase the oven temperature to 200°C/180°C fan/gas 6. Remove the thyme and bay leaves from the dish then gently stir in the chopped parsley and coriander. Spoon the casserole mixture into the pie dish.

Brush the edges of the chilled puff pastry with the egg yolk and cover the pie dish, pressing the pastry into the edge of the pie dish to seal. Cut a hole in the centre of the pastry then brush all over with the egg yolk. Place the pie back in the oven for 25–30 minutes until the pastry is a deep golden colour.

Serves: 4–6
Preparation time: 40 minutes
Cooking time: around 3 hours
   30 minutes

4 tbsp vegetable oil
4 tbsp plain flour
1½ tsp table salt
freshly ground black pepper
800g braising steak, cut into 2cm
   chunks
200g small shallots, peeled
2 tbsp tomato purée
2 garlic cloves, grated
¼ bunch of thyme, tied together with
   string
2 bay leaves
150g cooking chorizo, skin removed
   and sausagemeat diced into 1cm
   chunks
200ml ale
600ml Beef Stock (page 137)
1 tsp sweet smoked paprika
1 x 320g sheet ready-rolled all-butter
   puff pastry
2 tbsp finely chopped flat-leaf parsley
2 tbsp finely chopped coriander
2 egg yolks, beaten

Rib of beef has to be one of my favourite cuts. Ensure you buy dry-aged meat, as dry ageing allows the flavour to deepen and develop, and enhances the meat hugely. I would also recommend getting the forerib from a butcher rather than the supermarket, as the quality will be far superior. Bone marrow is something I remember from my childhood. It adds a wonderful richness and earthy flavour. *See image on following pages.*

RIB OF BEEF WITH RED WINE SAUCE, BONE MARROW AND YORKSHIRE PUDDINGS

Place the whole forerib in a clean plastic bag. Add the oil, herbs and garlic. Remove as much air from the bag as you can, then wrap it tightly in clingfilm. Leave it to marinate in the fridge for at least 24 hours, or up to 72 hours.

To make the red wine sauce, heat the vegetable oil in a large saucepan over high heat. Add the onion, carrot, celery and garlic to the pan and cook for about 5 minutes, stirring frequently, until soft and browned. Add the tomato purée, peppercorns and red wine. Bring to the boil, then simmer gently for 10–15 minutes until syrupy. Add the bay leaves, tarragon and beef stock and simmer for 30 minutes, skimming regularly to remove any fat. Strain the sauce through a fine sieve into a clean pan, then season to taste. Set aside; reheat before serving.

Preheat the oven to 200°C/180°C fan/gas 6.

To cook the beef, heat the oil from the marinade in a large, ovenproof frying pan over high heat until it's almost smoking. Season the marinated beef all over with table salt, then fry it in the pan for around 10 minutes, until browned on all sides. Add the butter and the herbs from the marinade. When the butter begins to foam, spoon it over the meat to baste. Baste for 10 minutes, constantly turning the rib over. Transfer the pan to the oven and cook for 30–40 minutes, basting and turning every 5 minutes. Check the core temperature of the beef with a meat thermometer and keep cooking until it reaches 38°C for rare. Remove the beef from the pan, cover with foil and leave somewhere warm to rest for at least 20 minutes while you cook the marrow and Yorkshire puddings.

Serves: 4
Preparation time: 15 minutes, plus 24–72 hours marinating
Cooking time: around 40 minutes

1 beef forerib (approx. 2.3kg)
50ml olive oil
4 sprigs of thyme
2 sprigs of rosemary
2 bay leaves
2 garlic cloves, peeled and crushed
1 tsp table salt
50g butter
sea salt and freshly ground black pepper

FOR THE RED WINE SAUCE
2 tbsp vegetable oil
1 onion, cut into large chunks
1 carrot, quartered
1 celery stick, quartered
2 garlic cloves, peeled and left whole
2 tbsp tomato purée
4 black peppercorns
250ml red wine
2 bay leaves
½ bunch of tarragon
400ml Beef Stock (page 137)
sea salt and freshly ground black pepper

While the beef is cooking, make the Yorkshire pudding batter. Weigh the eggs (in their shells) and measure out the same volume of flour and the same volume of milk. Crack the eggs into a deep bowl, add the flour and milk and blend with a stick blender. Pass through a fine sieve into a jug, to remove any lumps.

While the beef is resting, prepare the bone marrow. Mix the soft butter in a bowl with the table salt, tarragon and breadcrumbs. Season the marrow lightly and place the pieces on a baking tray in the oven for 10 minutes. Remove the tray from the oven and spoon the crumb onto each marrow. Drizzle with the vegetable oil and bake for a further 10–15 minutes.

To make the Yorkshire puddings, increase the oven temperature to 240°C/220°C fan/gas 8 (once the beef is cooked and resting). Place 12 Yorkshire pudding moulds or a 12-hole muffin tin on a tray. Fill each mould one-third full with vegetable oil and place the tray in the oven for 10 minutes for the oil to heat up.

When the oil is hot, open the oven and carefully pour the Yorkshire batter into the moulds, filling them to the top. Close the oven door and do not open it for 25 minutes. After 25 minutes, check the puddings to see if they are cooked through. Once cooked, very carefully remove the tray from the oven and set it on a heatproof surface. Remove the puddings from the oil as soon as you can touch them, and place them on a wire rack.

Carve the beef and serve with the bone marrow, hot red wine sauce and Yorkshire puddings.

FOR THE YORKSHIRE PUDDINGS
(MAKES 12)
4 eggs
plain flour
milk
1 tsp table salt
about 250ml vegetable oil

FOR THE BONE MARROW
30g soft butter
½ tsp table salt
1 tbsp finely chopped tarragon
50g panko breadcrumbs
4 pieces of bone marrow, cut
    lengthways so that the marrow is
    fully exposed
1 tbsp vegetable oil

Venison is not a cheap cut of meat but it is well worth it for a winter treat or special weekend meal for guests, when it is in season. If you are not a sprout fan, then you can substitute them with spinach instead.

LOIN OF VENISON WITH CREAMED SPROUTS AND JUNIPER SAUCE

Serves: 4
Preparation time: 20 minutes
Cooking time: about 1 hour

Heat half the vegetable oil in a large saucepan over high heat, then add the onion, celery, leek and carrot to the pan and fry for about 5 minutes, until lightly brown. Stir in the bay leaves and spices, then pour in the port, red wine, gin and vinegar. Bring to the boil, reduce the heat slightly and simmer for about 10 minutes to reduce the liquid by one-third.

Add the treacle and both stocks, return to the boil, then simmer for about 45 minutes, until the liquid has reduced to a thick, syrupy consistency. Strain the sauce through a sieve into a clean saucepan, season to taste with sea salt and pepper and keep hot.

To make the creamed sprouts, bring a large pan of salted water to the boil and blanch the sprouts for 3 minutes. Plunge in iced water and drain well. Put the double cream, thyme and bay leaves in a medium saucepan over medium heat and grate in all the nutmeg. Bring to the boil then reduce the heat and simmer for 10–15 minutes until the cream has reduced by half. Fish out the bay leaves and thyme sprigs, add the blanched sprouts and season to taste. Heat through until the sprouts are hot.

Preheat the oven to 180°C/160°C fan/gas 4.

Heat the remaining vegetable oil in a heavy-based frying pan over high heat. Season the venison all over, add it to the pan and fry for 5 minutes, until brown on all sides. Transfer to a roasting dish and put in the oven for 6–10 minutes, depending on the size of your pieces of venison. Remove from the oven and leave to rest for 5 minutes, then slice and serve with the creamed sprouts and juniper sauce.

4 tbsp vegetable oil
1 onion, quartered
2 celery sticks, quartered
1 leek, white part only, quartered
1 carrot, quartered
2 bay leaves
2 star anise
15 juniper berries
200ml port
100ml red wine
50ml gin
2 tbsp red wine vinegar
2 tbsp black treacle
300ml Beef Stock (page 137)
300ml Chicken Stock (page 83)
4 x 100–150g venison loin portions
    or steaks

FOR THE CREAMED SPROUTS
350g Brussels sprouts, brown leaves
    and stalks removed
150ml double cream
2 sprigs of thyme
2 bay leaves
½ nutmeg
sea salt and freshly ground black
    pepper

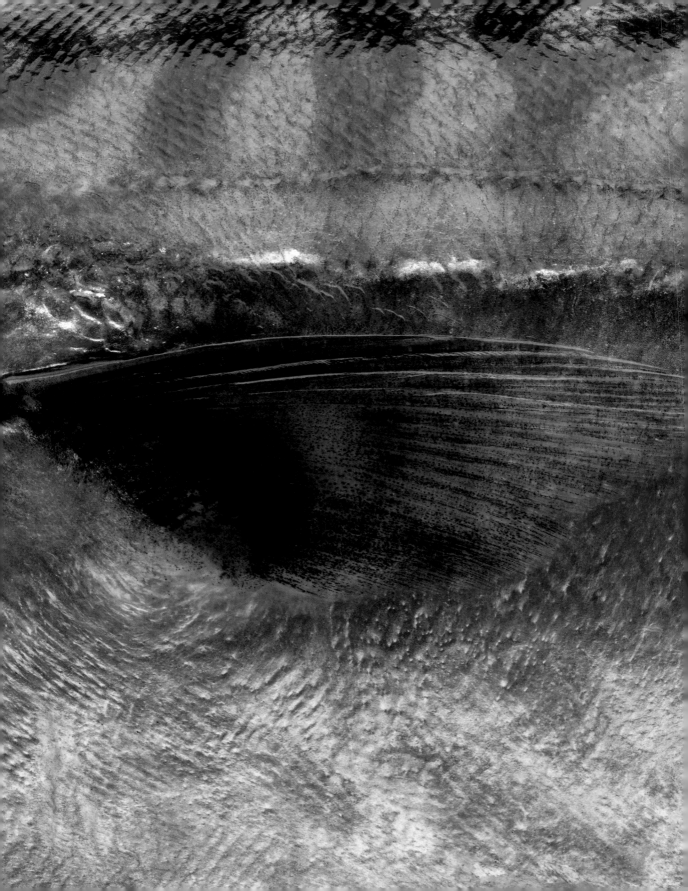

FROM THE SEA

This is a lovely light and healthy dish to add to your repertoire. The combination of sugar snap peas, kale and spring onions works really well with the sweetness of prawns, especially with the peanut and coriander.

PRAWN, SUGAR SNAP, KALE, PEANUT AND CORIANDER SALAD

To make the dressing, whisk all of the ingredients together in a bowl with 4 tablespoons of water and set aside.

To cook the prawns, heat a griddle pan over high heat until smoking. Drizzle the prawns with the oil and season with sea salt and pepper then cook on the griddle for about 1½ minutes on each side, or until cooked through.

Mix the sugar snap peas, kale, coriander and spring onions together in a bowl. Add the dressing and mix well. Place on a large serving platter then top with the prawns and peanuts.

Serves: 4
Preparation time: 15 minutes
Cooking time: 3 minutes

330g raw king prawns, peeled and
    veins removed
1 tbsp vegetable oil
150g sugar snap peas, thinly sliced
200g trimmed kale, finely sliced
½ bunch of coriander, leaves chopped
½ bunch of spring onions, finely sliced
80g roasted peanuts, chopped
sea salt and freshly ground black
    pepper

FOR THE DRESSING
3 tbsp toasted sesame oil
1 tbsp soy sauce
½ tbsp runny honey
2 tbsp rice wine vinegar
½ green chilli, deseeded and finely
    diced
1 tbsp peanut butter

This chilled tomato soup is based on an Andalusian recipe with some additional touches. It is thickened with bread and almonds and is absolutely delicious. You need to use ripe and flavoursome tomatoes, otherwise the end result will be a little bland. The soup is also delicious on its own for a summer lunch.

CRAB WITH CHILLED TOMATO SOUP, LEMON AND PICKLED CUCUMBER

To make the soup, cut the tomatoes into 1cm-thick slices and place them on a tray in a single layer. Sprinkle generously with sea salt and pepper then transfer to the freezer for 1 hour. Defrost and transfer to a colander placed over a bowl to collect the juice (no need to press them to extract juice). Add the bread to the juice and leave for 20 minutes. Set the tomatoes aside.

Place the soaked bread and the other soup ingredients into a blender or food processor with the tomatoes and blitz until smooth. Pass through a fine sieve into a bowl or large jug and adjust seasoning to taste. Chill immediately.

To make the lemon confit, dissolve the sugar in 50ml boiling water then pour it over the lemon pieces in a bowl. Leave to cool.

To make the pickled cucumber, whisk the vinegar and honey together. Place the cucumber rounds in a shallow dish and pour over the pickle mix. Allow to sit at room temperature for 30 minutes.

Mix the crab meat in a bowl with the olive oil and lemon juice and season to taste.

To serve, pour the soup into four bowls then garnish with the crab meat, lemon confit and pickled cucumber. Top with a generous drizzle of extra virgin olive oil and small basil leaves.

Serves: 4 as a starter
Preparation time: 25 minutes, plus 1 hour freezing, 30 minutes pickling and 1 hour chilling

FOR THE TOMATO SOUP
500g very ripe plum tomatoes
1 slice of bread (sourdough works well), crusts removed, diced (approx. 50g)
25g flaked almonds, toasted
¼ cucumber, peeled and diced
1 shallot, finely sliced
3 basil leaves, torn
small handful of coriander leaves
25g tomato purée
125ml tomato juice, plus extra to loosen if needed
½ tsp sweet smoked paprika
1 tbsp sherry vinegar
25ml extra virgin olive oil
sea salt and freshly ground black pepper
small basil leaves, to serve

FOR THE LEMON CONFIT
1 tbsp caster sugar
½ lemon, segmented then sliced into 4 (peel on)

FOR THE PICKLED CUCUMBER
50ml white wine vinegar
1 tbsp runny honey
¼ cucumber, cut into 2mm-thick rounds

FOR THE CRAB
100g white crab meat
1 tbsp extra virgin olive oil, plus a little extra to drizzle
juice of ½ lemon

Fish soup is traditionally made with roasted fish bones, however I have made this version using ingredients that are easier to get hold of. You can substitute any similar fish for the sea bass: sea bream works well, as does hake. The Provençal dish Bouillabaisse is traditionally served with rouille, a garlicky saffron aioli, and my version really lifts the flavours of this dish even more.

FISH SOUP WITH SEA BASS, MACKEREL AND PRAWNS

To make the soup, heat 2 tablespoons of the vegetable oil in a large saucepan over high heat. Add the onion, fennel, carrot, celery, leek and garlic and fry for about 15 minutes until they start to turn golden. Remove them from the pan and place in a dish then add another 2 tablespoons of the oil to the pan. When hot, add the prawn shells and fry until golden. Add the tomato purée and cook for 2 minutes then return the browned vegetables to the pan. Add the white wine and brandy and simmer until the liquid is reduced to a syrup. Add the saffron, star anise, bay leaves, tomatoes, fish stock, vegetable stock and paprika and simmer gently for 20 minutes.

Pass the soup through a fine sieve into a clean saucepan, pressing down with the base of a ladle to extract as much of the liquid and flavour as possible. Place the pan over medium heat and let it simmer for 10–15 minutes until slightly reduced. Season to taste.

Meanwhile, make the rouille. Place all ingredients, except the olive oil, in a blender or food processor and blitz until smooth. Gradually drizzle in the olive oil, with the blade still turning, until a thick mayonnaise is formed. Season to taste and set aside.

Heat another 2 tablespoons of vegetable oil in a large, non-stick frying pan over medium-high heat. When hot, pat the sea bass dry, season and place skin side down in the pan. Cook for 3–4 minutes, until golden and crispy, then gently turn to cook the other side, removing the pan from the heat. Remove from the pan to rest. Do the same with the mackerel fillets, adding the remaining tablespoon of oil if needed. Season the prawns then add them to the pan and cook for about 1½ minutes on each side until golden.

To serve, pour the soup into four bowls. Divide the sea bass, mackerel and prawns between each bowl and serve with a dollop of the rouille.

Serves: 4
Preparation time: 30 minutes
Cooking time: around 1 hour 20 minutes

12 prawns, peeled and veins removed
2 sea bass fillets, skin on, pin-boned, scored and halved
2 large mackerel fillets, skin on, pin-boned, scored and halved

FOR THE SOUP
6–7 tbsp vegetable oil
1 onion, roughly diced
1 fennel bulb, chopped
1 carrot, chopped
1 celery stick, chopped
1 leek, white part only, chopped
1 garlic bulb, halved horizontally
2 tsp tomato purée
200ml white wine
50ml brandy
pinch of saffron strands
2 star anise
2 bay leaves
5 plum tomatoes, chopped
1 litre Fish Stock (page 177)
300ml Vegetable Stock (page 57)
½ tsp sweet smoked paprika

FOR THE ROUILLE
2 garlic cloves, finely grated
pinch of saffron threads
3 egg yolks
½ tsp cayenne pepper
1 tbsp tomato purée
50g piquillo peppers (from a jar or tin), drained
grated zest and juice of ½–1 lemon (to taste)
20g stale bread
150ml extra virgin olive oil
sea salt and freshly ground black pepper

When I first started working as a chef at the Savoy Hotel we used to make around 10 sides of gravadlax per week, for the salmon trolley. The gravadlax would be carved by the waiters in the dining room, in front of the guests. It was a remarkable sight to watch the waiters' skills back in the day of carving in the dining room. Regardless of how you slice it, this gravadlax is great for salads, with sourdough or as a canapé.

GRAVADLAX WITH GRAPEFRUIT AND CORIANDER

Place the rock salt, sugar, grapefruit, coriander, juniper berries and gin in a blender or food processor and pulse until a thick paste is formed.

Place the salmon in a container that will fit in your fridge and will not get tainted by the marinade. Smother the paste all over the salmon. Cover and chill for 48 hours, turning the salmon over after 24 hours.

Wash the marinade off the fish thoroughly under cold running water and pat the salmon dry with kitchen paper. Slice thinly and serve.

Serves: 6
Preparation time: 5 minutes,
    plus 48 hours curing

100g rock salt
50g demerara sugar
1 pink grapefruit, quartered
1 bunch of coriander
1 tbsp juniper berries
75ml gin
½ side of salmon, skin on, pin-boned,
    skin scored (about 500g)

Brown shrimps, or Morecambe Bay shrimps, are small, sweet shrimps that are harvested near Southport, where I grew up. They are readily available in supermarkets nowadays and you don't have to do much to them to enjoy them.

BROWN SHRIMPS, BROAD BEANS, FENNEL AND LEMON BRUSCHETTA

Bring a medium saucepan of salted water to the boil, add the broad beans and blanch them for 3 minutes. Drain and refresh under cold running water then drain well.

Melt the butter in a large frying pan over medium-high heat. When hot, add the shrimps and toss to coat. Add the lemon zest and juice, and the mace and season well with sea salt and pepper. Add the blanched broad beans and toss to coat. Finish with the parsley and remove the pan from the heat.

Mix the white wine vinegar and olive oil together then toss with the sliced fennel in a bowl. Season well.

Toast the bread slices lightly on each side then place one slice on each plate. Top each slice with a quarter of the shrimp mix and the fennel salad.

Serves: 4 as a starter
Preparation time: 10 minutes
Cooking time: 5 minutes

100g podded broad beans
50g butter
180g brown shrimps
grated zest and juice of 1 lemon
¼ tsp ground mace
1 tbsp finely chopped flat-leaf parsley
2 tbsp white wine vinegar
1 tbsp olive oil
1 fennel bulb, finely sliced
4 slices brown bread
sea salt and freshly ground black
    pepper

Tuna crudo, or tartare, is such a fresh dish that it needs a little acidity and sweetness to finish it. Ensure your tuna is as fresh as possible and always keep it chilled. Season it just before serving, otherwise the salt will draw the moisture out of the fish.

TUNA CRUDO WITH MISO, APPLE, LIME AND SAMPHIRE

Start by making the dressing. Whisk the lime juice and zest in a bowl with the miso paste until combined, then whisk in the olive oil and palm sugar.

Cut the tuna into thin slices and divide between four plates. Slice the apple as thinly as possible. Combine the apple and samphire with half of the dressing just prior to serving. Season with black pepper and sea salt if needed.

Add the apple and samphire to the plates, and drizzle the tuna with the remaining dressing.

Serves: 4 as a starter
Preparation time: 10 minutes

300g sushi-grade fresh tuna
1 Granny Smith apple
100g raw samphire (tender, slim
    stems only), to serve
sea salt and freshly ground black
    pepper

FOR THE DRESSING
grated zest and juice of 1–2 limes, to
    taste
½ tsp white miso paste
2 tbsp extra virgin olive oil
½ tsp palm sugar, grated (or in
    pieces)

This chilli and coriander salsa works well with any fish or seafood dish and is a great complement to the sweetness of scallops. It is vibrant green and tangy and has a wonderful, almost addictive, aroma and flavour. Try to source large scallops from your fishmonger – the best ones come from Scotland.

GRILLED SCALLOPS WITH GREEN CHILLI AND CORIANDER SALSA, PEACH AND BUTTERMILK

Put the buttermilk in a sieve lined with a piece of muslin cloth and place the sieve over a bowl. Put the sieve and bowl in the fridge for 6 hours. Scrape the strained buttermilk out of the muslin cloth, put it into a clean bowl and whisk it.

To make the salsa, blend all the ingredients together in a small food processor, or in a jug or bowl with a stick blender, until smooth. Season to taste with sea salt and pepper.

Heat the vegetable oil in a large frying pan over high heat. Season the scallops. When the oil in the pan is almost smoking, place the scallops in the pan, one by one, in a clockwise configuration. As soon as you have put the last scallop in the pan, start turning the first scallop over, then continue one by one in the same clockwise direction. They'll be done after about a minute or so on each side. Remove from the pan.

To serve, divide the salsa between 4 plates then arrange the scallops and peach slices on top. Add a dollop of the strained buttermilk and sprinkle over the coriander cress or coriander leaves.

Serves: 4
Preparation time: 10 minutes, plus
    6 hours straining
Cooking time: less than 5 minutes

120ml buttermilk
1 tbsp vegetable oil
12 medium or 6 large scallops, roe
    removed
1 ripe peach, halved and cut into
    3mm-thick slices
sea salt and freshly ground black
    pepper
coriander cress or small coriander
    leaves, to serve

FOR THE GREEN CHILLI AND
CORIANDER SALSA
grated zest and juice of 1 lime
1 garlic clove, finely grated
1 small green chilli, deseeded and
    roughly chopped
2 tbsp rice wine vinegar
1 tbsp chopped coriander
1 tbsp chopped mint
1 tbsp chopped dill
6 large basil leaves
60ml olive oil

This may seem like an unusual recipe but it is absolutely delicious and works well for a weekend brunch or lunch. You can use any bread you have in the house, as it works well with sourdough-style breads as well as white bread.

PRAWN FRENCH TOAST

Preheat the oven to 200°C/180°C fan/gas 6 and line a baking tray with foil.

Mix together all the ingredients for the prawn filling in a bowl.

Divide the prawn mixture between four slices of bread and top with the grated Gruyère. Place the other plain slices of bread on top and flatten.

Whisk together the eggs and cream in a wide, shallow bowl and soak the sandwiches in the mix for 5 minutes on each side.

Heat 25g of the butter in a large frying pan over medium-high heat. When foaming, place two sandwiches at a time in the pan and fry for about 5 minutes until they start to brown, then carefully turn them over and fry for a further 5 minutes. Remove from the heat, add the remaining butter to the pan and repeat with the remaining two sandwiches. Transfer the fried sandwiches to the foil-lined tray and drizzle with any remaining butter. Bake for 8–10 minutes until golden and the prawn filling is cooked through.

Serves: 4
Preparation time: 15 minutes, plus
    10 minutes soaking
Cooking time: 40 minutes

8 medium slices of bread
100g grated Gruyère cheese
2 eggs, beaten
2 tbsp double cream
40g butter

FOR THE PRAWN FILLING
165g raw king prawns, peeled, veins
    removed and prawns finely
    chopped
½ red chilli, deseeded and finely
    chopped
2 tbsp toasted sesame oil
2.5cm piece of fresh ginger, peeled
    and finely grated
1 garlic clove, finely grated
6 basil leaves, finely chopped
grated zest of ½ lime
½ tsp table salt

HOT SMOKING

Smoking is a cooking technique that has had a resurgence of late. Cold smoking means only applying enough heat to start the mix smouldering so that smoke permeates the produce with flavour, rather than cooking it. Hot smoking, however, involves applying further heat to cook the food as well as flavour it, and was traditionally used as a method of preserving foods, mainly meat and fish.

In the restaurants we tend to use a mix of wood chips, tea leaves, herbs, pine needles and hay to create smoke. For home smoking, I find tea, or hardy herbs, combined with sugar and rice to keep it alight, is the best smoke mix. You can purchase smoking trays, if you are intending to use this technique regularly. Alternatively, an old roasting tray, or baking tin, with a wire rack and covered with foil works well. However, note that it is hard to get the scent off the tray and rack once you have used them for smoking.

It is important to season the food you are smoking before you smoke it. Fish can also be slightly cured first, in a mix of demerara sugar and rock salt, to enhance the flavour (rinsing the cure off under cold running water and patting dry, before smoking).

Do bear in mind that smoke alarms will react so ensure, when you remove the lid or foil, that your kitchen is well ventilated. Remove the foil slowly, to let the smoke escape gradually so as not to 'smoke out' your kitchen. Alternatively, if you can, take the dish outside to remove the foil, so the smoke dissipates in the air. If you want a heavier smoke flavour, leave the foil on for longer.

SMOKE MIX

Preheat the oven to 110°C/90°C fan/gas ¼. Line a roasting tray or baking tin with foil and scatter over the smoke mix. Place a wire rack on top, making sure the bottom isn't touching the rice. Place the ingredients you want to smoke on the rack, in a single layer. Cover the entire wire rack and tray with a tent of foil, leaving one corner open so you can see inside. Place the covered tray on a medium-high heat until you see smoke (approximately 3 minutes), then carefully seal the foil tightly so no smoke will escape, and turn off the heat. Leave the tin sealed for 2 minutes and then place in the preheated oven for the length of time shown below.

1 tsp demerara sugar

2 tbsp white rice

1 tsp tea leaves

2 tbsp herbs/3 leaves/3 sprigs

PRODUCE	SMOKING MATERIAL	TIME IN OVEN
Small fish fillets (1.5cm or thinner)	Chamomile tea, black tea, Earl Grey tea, pine needles, lavender, bay leaves	8 minutes
Large fish fillets (2cm or thicker)	Chamomile tea, black tea, Earl Grey tea, pine needles, lavender, bay leaves	12 minutes
Chicken breast, duck breast	Black tea, Earl Grey tea, rosemary, pine needles, thyme, bay leaves	10 minutes
Carrots, parsnips	Chamomile tea, pine needles, lavender, rosemary, thyme	20 minutes
Potatoes, celeriac	Chamomile tea, pine needles, lavender, rosemary, thyme	25 minutes
Fruit	Chamomile tea, mint, lavender, bay leaves, rosemary	10 minutes

Smoked mackerel is the ideal showcase for hot smoking. I really like the sweetness of the baked lemon jam with the smoky, oily mackerel in this recipe. It's is a great condiment to keep in your fridge and works with any fish and seafood and is pretty straightforward to make, yet has an interesting caramelised flavour.

ROSEMARY SMOKED MACKEREL WITH BAKED LEMON JAM, FENNEL AND CRÈME FRAÎCHE

Preheat the oven to 220°C/200°C fan/gas 7 and line a baking dish with foil.

To make the baked lemon jam, put the lemons in the foil-lined dish and bake for 30–40 minutes, turning them a few times until they are a deep golden colour. Remove from the oven, place the lemons in a blender or food processor with the sugar, olive oil and 2 tablespoons of water (plus any juice that might have seeped out into the baking dish). Blend until smooth, adding a little more water if needed, to form a thick jam. Pass through a fine sieve into a bowl, to remove any lumps.

Smoke the mackerel according to the method on page 165, drizzling the flesh of the mackerel with the vegetable oil, seasoning it with salt and placing the fillets, skin side down, on the rack (you may need to smoke them in batches), in a single layer. When you see smoke, seal the tin and place in the oven for 8 minutes. Remove from the oven and set aside (with the foil intact) for a further 5 minutes, before carefully removing the foil.

Mix the crème fraîche in a bowl with the lemon zest and season with sea salt and pepper.

Just before you are ready to serve, dress the fennel by placing the bulb slices and chopped fronds in a bowl, adding the olive oil, lemon zest and juice. Season to taste. Don't do this too far in advance otherwise the fennel will turn limp with the acid of the lemon juice and the salt.

To serve, dot the baked lemon jam around the plates, adding a spoonful of the crème fraîche. Place 2 fillets of smoked mackerel on each plate then finish with the fennel salad.

Serves: 4
Preparation time: 20 minutes
Cooking time: around 45 minutes

1 x quantity of Smoke Mix (page 165), using 3 sprigs of rosemary
8 mackerel fillets, pin-boned
2 tbsp vegetable oil
100g crème fraîche
grated zest of ½ lemon
sea salt and freshly ground black pepper

FOR THE BAKED LEMON JAM
2 lemons
3 tbsp caster sugar
2 tbsp olive oil

FOR THE FENNEL
1 fennel bulb with fronds, bulb finely sliced and fronds finely chopped
2 tbsp olive oil
grated zest and juice of ½ lemon

Eggs Benedict is the perfect brunch or weekend lunch dish. I enjoy it more with hot smoked salmon, as in this recipe, as I feel it works so well with soft-poached eggs and loads of hollandaise. The secret to making hollandaise is to not let the egg yolks get too hot, then to add the butter little by little, until it emulsifies.

HOT SMOKED SALMON EGGS BENEDICT

Preheat the oven to 130°C/110°C fan/gas ¾.

To make the hollandaise reduction, put all the ingredients in a saucepan and bring to the boil. Cook for 6–8 minutes until only a third of the liquid remains. Strain the liquid through a sieve into a jug and discard the shallots and herbs.

Combine the demerara sugar and the rock salt and liberally coat the salmon portions in the mixture. Leave to cure for 10 minutes, then rinse the salmon thoroughly under cold running water and pat dry with kitchen paper.

Smoke the fish according to the method on page 165. When you see smoke, seal the tin and transfer to the oven for 8–12 minutes, depending on how thick your salmon fillets are. Remove from the oven and set aside for 5 minutes, then gently remove the foil, taking care to let the smoke escape gradually. Lift out the salmon and set aside.

To make the hollandaise, begin by melting the butter. When melted, the butter will split so that white milk solids sink below the yellow liquid. Place the egg yolks in a large, stainless-steel or heatproof glass bowl. Bring ⅓ of a pan of water to a very gentle simmer. Place the bowl of egg yolks over the steaming pan and whisk until they are thick and ribbons form when you lift the whisk (it's easiest to do this with an electric whisk). Very slowly add a little of the yellow clarified butter, whisking continuously. Keep adding a small amount of the butter, whisking well between additions then, when the hollandaise begins to thicken, add 3 tablespoons of the reduction, then continue adding the butter. Discard the milk solids. Season to taste with sea salt then cover and set aside.

Serves: 4

Preparation time: 35 minutes, plus 10 minutes curing

Cooking time: around 20 minutes, plus 8-12 minutes smoking

2 tbsp demerara sugar
2 tbsp rock salt
2 skinless and boneless salmon fillet portions (about 150g each)
1 x quantity of Smoke Mix (page 165), using 1 tsp Earl Grey tea leaves
220g butter
3 egg yolks
4 English muffins, halved
sea salt and freshly ground black pepper

FOR THE HOLLANDAISE REDUCTION
2 shallots, peeled and sliced
1 bay leaf
100ml white wine
3 sprigs of thyme
40ml white wine vinegar
¼ tsp fennel seeds

To poach the eggs, boil a large saucepan of water with a heavy pinch of salt. Crack half of the eggs into four separate bowls and add a few drops of vinegar to each. Whisk the boiling water so it swirls in a whirlpool, turn the heat down so the water is at a gentle simmer then slide in the eggs. Poach for 3–4 minutes, remove with a slotted spoon and place on a warm plate. Repeat with the other 4 eggs.

Toast the muffins. Flake the salmon into large chunks and place it on top of the muffins. Add an egg to each muffin, on top of the salmon, then smother with the hollandaise. Sprinkle with a liberal twist of black pepper.

FOR THE SOFT-POACHED EGGS
8 eggs
½ tsp white wine vinegar

Tacos to me used to mean the crispy shells filled with mince, beans and cheese. Times have changed and it's great to learn about more authentic ways of cooking Mexican food. My version of fish tacos makes a great midweek supper. I like to salt the fish first as it seasons it well and also helps remove any excess moisture, but it's not essential.

FISH TACOS

Serves: 4–6
Preparation time: 20 minutes, plus
    2 hours pickling
Cooking time: less than 10 minutes

To make the pickled chilli and onion rings, place the caster sugar in a pan with the mustard seeds and 100ml water. Bring to the boil then reduce the heat and simmer until the sugar has dissolved. Remove from the heat, add the vinegar and mix well. Add the onion rings and chopped chilli. Cover and set aside at room temperature for a minimum of 2 hours.

Cover the fish with rock salt, if using, and leave for 10 minutes, then thoroughly rinse off the salt under cold running water and pat the fish dry with kitchen paper.

Mix the sour cream, mayonnaise and harissa paste together in a bowl, cover and chill until ready to serve.

Pour enough vegetable oil into a large, deep frying pan to come up to approximately 1cm and place on medium heat (160°C on a thermometer). Place the flour, beaten eggs and panko breadcrumbs in three separate bowls. Coat the fish pieces in the flour, dust off the excess, then dip them in the beaten egg and finish them with a coating of the panko breadcrumbs.

To fry the fish, place the pieces gently in the hot oil in batches for 4–6 minutes until golden and cooked through. Carefully remove each piece of fish from the pan with a large slotted spoon and place on sheets of kitchen paper to absorb excess oil.

Heat a dry frying pan and toast each taco for 10 seconds on each side, to warm them through.

Add the coriander to the pickled onion rings.

Add 2 pieces of fish to each taco, top with shredded lettuce, grated radish, pickled chilli and onion and harissa sour cream.

4 skinless cod fillets or other firm-
    fleshed white fish (about 150g per
    portion), each cut into 3 pieces
100g rock salt (optional)
vegetable oil, for shallow-frying
50–60g plain flour, for dusting
3 eggs, beaten
200g panko breadcrumbs
12 small, soft tacos, or 6 large tortillas
2 Baby Gem lettuces, washed and
    finely shredded
1 bunch of round radishes, washed
    and grated

FOR THE PICKLED CHILLI AND
ONION RINGS
50g caster sugar
1 tbsp yellow mustard seeds
100ml white wine vinegar
1 onion, finely sliced into rings
1 green chilli, deseeded if you wish,
    finely chopped
½ bunch of coriander, leaves finely
    chopped

FOR THE HARISSA SOUR CREAM
160g sour cream
1 tbsp good-quality mayonnaise
1 tsp harissa paste

When I first started working as a chef, one of my big jobs was slicing onions Lyonnaise. Each slice had to be the same thickness, onion after onion. While you do not have to be as precise as I did, the more similar in size your onion slices are, the more evenly they will cook.

SEARED TUNA WITH LYONNAISE ONIONS, PINE NUTS AND PICKLED CARROTS

To make the pickled carrots, place the vinegar, caster sugar and mustard seeds in a medium saucepan with 100ml water. Bring to the boil, then remove from the heat and allow to cool. When it has reached room temperature, add the carrots and cover. Leave to marinate at room temperature for at least 1 hour.

Meanwhile, make the Lyonnaise onions. Melt the butter in a large saucepan over medium heat. Add the sliced onions and thyme sprigs and season well. Cook until the onions begin to caramelise, stirring frequently, then reduce the heat to low and continue to cook for about 30 minutes until the onions are glossy and sticky. Remove from the heat and discard the thyme sprigs. When cool, add the olive oil, balsamic vinegar and chopped pine nuts.

Heat a non-stick frying pan over high heat. Pat the tuna steaks dry with kitchen paper and season one side of each with sea salt and pepper. Add just enough oil to cover the base of the frying pan and heat until the oil is shimmering. Place the tuna steaks seasoned side down in the hot oil, then season the top with sea salt and pepper. Reduce the heat to medium-high and leave to cook, undisturbed, for 1 minute. Flip the tuna over with a fish slice and cook for a further minute, undisturbed. Remove from the pan and leave to rest for a couple of minutes.

Cut each steak across the grain into approximately 5mm-thick slices and arrange them on top of the Lyonnaise onions. Serve with the pickled carrots and scatter with parsley.

Serves: 4
Preparation time: 15 minutes, plus
    1 hour marinating
Cooking time: around 35 minutes

4 tuna steaks (about 150g each)
vegetable oil, for searing
micro parsley, or finely chopped flat-
    leaf parsley, to serve

FOR THE LYONNAISE ONIONS
40g butter
2 large onions, finely sliced
3 sprigs of thyme
2 tbsp extra virgin olive oil
1 tsp good-quality balsamic vinegar
30g pine nuts, toasted and roughly
    chopped
sea salt and freshly ground black
    pepper

FOR THE PICKLED CARROTS
50ml white wine vinegar
30g caster sugar
½ tsp yellow mustard seeds
2 medium carrots, finely sliced or
    peeled to make strips

A fish goujon is basically a grown-up version of a fish finger. I really like adding Parmesan and paprika to the crumb as they contribute so much to the overall flavour. And you just cannot beat homemade tartare sauce, loaded with capers, gherkins and herbs. I like to salt fish before cooking it for two reasons: firstly, it seasons the flesh more intensely, and secondly, it removes any excess moisture. Always ensure you rinse the salt off fully, and pat the fish dry before cooking.

COD GOUJONS WITH PARMESAN CRUMB AND TARTARE SAUCE

If you want to salt the fish before cooking it, put the cod strips in a shallow bowl, cover them with rock salt and leave for 5 minutes. Thoroughly rinse off the salt with cold water and pat the fish dry with kitchen paper.

Pour enough vegetable oil in a deep-fat fryer or deep saucepan to come halfway up the pan and heat to 160°C.

While the oil is heating up, make the tartare sauce. Put the egg yolks, vinegar, mustard and a pinch of salt in a bowl and combine with a balloon whisk. Combine the olive oil and vegetable oil in a jug. Slowly, a few drips at a time at the beginning, drizzle the oil into the egg mixture, whisking continuously until the sauce is thick. Alternatively, use a small blender. Stir in the squeeze of lemon, capers, gherkins, parsley and tarragon. Taste and add salt if necessary.

Prepare the coating for the goujons by putting the seasoned flour in one bowl, the beaten eggs in another and mixing the breadcrumbs with the paprika and Parmesan in a third bowl.

Coat the cod strips in the seasoned flour, dust off any excess, then dip them into the egg and finish them with a generous coating of Parmesan breadcrumbs.

To fry the cod goujons, carefully drop them into the hot oil and fry for 5–6 minutes until deep golden and crisp. Carefully remove the goujons from the pan with a large slotted spoon and place on sheets of kitchen paper to absorb excess oil. Fry the remaining goujons and serve immediately with a good dollop of the tartare sauce.

Serves: 4
Preparation time: 20 minutes
Cooking time: 5–6 minutes

4 skinless cod fillets (about 150g each), sliced into 1.5–2cm-thick strips
rock salt (enough to coat the cod strips) (optional)
vegetable oil, for deep-frying
75g plain flour, seasoned with sea salt and freshly ground black pepper
3 eggs, beaten
200g dried breadcrumbs (preferably panko breadcrumbs)
1 tsp sweet smoked paprika
100g Parmesan, grated

FOR THE TARTARE SAUCE
3 egg yolks
1 tbsp white wine vinegar
½ tsp Dijon mustard
175ml olive oil
50ml vegetable oil
squeeze of lemon juice
2 tbsp finely chopped capers
2 tbsp finely chopped gherkins
1 tbsp finely chopped flat-leaf parsley
1 tbsp finely chopped tarragon
sea salt, to taste

Halibut is one of my favourite fish. It has a robust flavour with a lovely, flaky texture. It is the largest flat fish available, therefore the fillets are often relatively thick. To serve four people you may only need half a side, which is one fillet, given its large size. You'll probably find you have some hazelnut and thyme pesto left over, in which case store it in the fridge and use it as a garnish for soup, in a salad, or just with crusty bread.

ROAST HALIBUT WITH MUSHROOM VELOUTÉ AND THYME PESTO

To make the mushroom velouté, start by melting the butter in a large, wide saucepan until it begins to froth. Add the onion, garlic, thyme and bay leaf. Season well with sea salt and pepper. Cook over medium heat for 15–20 minutes, stirring frequently, until the onion is golden and caramelised.

Increase the heat to medium-high, add the mushrooms and cook for 10–15 minutes, until any liquid that seeps out of the mushrooms has almost cooked away. Add the stock and simmer gently for 10 minutes. Remove the thyme stalks and bay leaf. Purée the velouté in a blender until smooth, then add the cream and whizz again. Stir in the sherry vinegar, taste and add a little more seasoning, if you like.

To make the pesto, put all ingredients in a food processor and pulse-blend until you have a chunky pesto consistency. Season to taste.

To cook the halibut, heat the oil in a large non-stick frying pan. Season the fish on both sides then place the portions gently in the pan. Cook on medium-high heat for 3–4 minutes on one side until golden, then carefully turn the fish over and colour the other side. Add the butter and cook for a further 2 minutes until the fish is cooked through, frequently basting it with the melted butter.

To serve, spoon mushroom velouté in the bottom of each bowl. Place the fish on top and finish with a spoonful of pesto. Top each serving with the extra thyme leaves.

Serves: 4
Preparation time: 20 minutes
Cooking time: around 50 minutes

2 tbsp vegetable oil
4 halibut portions (160–180g each)
25g butter

FOR THE MUSHROOM VELOUTÉ
25g butter
1 onion, sliced
1 garlic clove, crushed
¼ bunch of thyme, plus extra picked
    leaves to serve
1 bay leaf
250g field (flat) mushrooms, sliced
300ml Chicken or Vegetable Stock
    (pages 83 and 57)
50ml double cream
splash of sherry vinegar
sea salt and freshly ground black
    pepper

FOR THE HAZELNUT AND
THYME PESTO
100g blanched hazelnuts
100ml olive oil, plus extra if needed
25g grated Parmesan cheese
1 tbsp thyme leaves

Traditionally, gratins are made with a white sauce. My twist is using tomato as a base, meaning the gratin is slightly lighter but just as delicious. You can use any mix of seafood you like, such as smoked fish or mussels. Do try to make your own fish stock, too; it is very quick to make and the flavour will be much fresher and cleaner than shop-bought varieties.

SEAFOOD GRATIN WITH TOMATO AND BASIL

Start by making the sauce. Heat the oil in a large saucepan over medium-high heat. When hot, add the onions, garlic and a good pinch of sea salt and cook, stirring frequently, for about 10 minutes until soft but not coloured. Add the chilli and wine and increase the heat to high. When the wine is boiling, add the clams or cockles to the pan and cover. Cook for 2 minutes or until the shells have opened, then remove the pan from the heat and pick out all the clams or cockles using tongs. Allow to cool then pick the meat out of the shells.

Cut the white fish into roughly 2cm chunks. Cover them in the rock salt and leave for 5 minutes, then rinse under cold running water and pat dry with kitchen paper.

Melt the butter in a large saucepan over medium heat. Whisk in the flour until smooth and cook over low heat for 2 minutes, stirring constantly. Gradually whisk in the fish or vegetable stock, followed by the tomato purée and whisk well. Add the chopped tomatoes and mix until combined. Add the cooked onions and wine mixture to the tomato mix and bring to a boil, then reduce the heat to low and simmer for 5 minutes, stirring regularly, until thickened. Remove from the heat, season to taste and stir through the basil.

Preheat the oven to 210°C/190°C fan/gas 7.

To make the crumb, place the butter in a bowl and beat until smooth. Add the chopped parsley, lemon zest and grated nutmeg and mix well. Mix in the panko breadcrumbs using your fingers, so that the crumbs are coated in the butter. Season to taste.

Serves: 4
Preparation time: 30 minutes
Cooking time: around 40 minutes

3 skinless white fish fillets, such as pollock, hake or haddock (approx. 180g each)
3 tbsp rock salt
200g raw jumbo king prawns, peeled and veins removed

FOR THE SAUCE
2 tbsp vegetable oil
2 onions, finely sliced
2 garlic cloves, crushed
½ red chilli, deseeded and finely diced
200ml white wine
500g raw white clams or cockles, cleaned
60g butter
60g plain flour
350ml warm Fish or Vegetable Stock (pages 177 and 57)
2 tbsp tomato purée
1 x 400g tin chopped tomatoes
1 bunch of basil, leaves finely chopped
sea salt and freshly ground black pepper

Place half the tomato mix in a 20cm square casserole dish. Cover with the fish, prawns and clams. Top with the remaining tomato mix then sprinkle the crumb on top. Bake for around 20 minutes until golden then serve immediately.

FOR THE CRUMB
30g soft butter
3 tbsp chopped flat-leaf parsley
grated zest of 1 lemon
generous grating of nutmeg
100g panko breadcrumbs

FISH STOCK

Roughly chop the fish bones and put them in a bowl or pan of cold water to soak for about 10 minutes. Drain and set aside.

Heat the olive oil in a large stock pot. Add the onion, leek, celery, garlic, bay leaf, parsley, coriander seeds, peppercorns and star anise. Cook over low heat for about 5 minutes until the vegetables start to soften.

Increase the heat, pour in the wine and boil until the wine has reduced by half. Stir in the fish bones and 2 litres of water. Bring to the boil, skim any discoloured foam/scum from the surface, reduce the heat to low and simmer gently for 30 minutes, skimming occasionally.

Strain the stock through a colander and then through a fine sieve. Use the stock straight away or cool and chill in the fridge for 3–4 days. Alternatively, freeze and use within 4 months.

Makes: approx. 1.5 litres
Preparation time: 20 minutes
Cooking time: 3 hours

1.5kg fish bones, with heads, but eyes and gills removed
5 tbsp olive oil
1 onion, chopped
1 leek, white part only, chopped
2 celery sticks, chopped
1 garlic bulb, halved
1 bay leaf
a few parsley stalks
10 coriander seeds
5 white peppercorns
1 star anise
300ml dry white wine

Szechuan pepper has a unique flavour and an aromatic quality that can be quite addictive. However, if you go overboard you will end up with numb lips! When purchasing fish always look for bright, shiny skin – it should not be dull and rubbery.

SZECHUAN-SPICED SEA BREAM WITH RADISH SLAW

Heat 1 tablespoon of the vegetable oil in a medium frying pan over medium-high heat. When hot, add the onion and crushed Szechuan peppercorns. Cook for 7–10 minutes until golden and fragrant, stirring frequently. Add the sherry and cook for 1 minute, then add the sesame oil, soy sauce and chopped peanuts. Mix well, remove from the heat and set aside.

To make the slaw, combine in a bowl the sesame oil with the rice wine vinegar, coriander and pickled ginger. Add the radish rounds, season well with sea salt and set aside.

To cook the sea bream, heat the remaining vegetable oil in a large, non-stick frying pan. When hot, season the bream then place the fillets in the pan, skin side down, pressing down on them lightly for a few moments with your fingers, to keep them from curling. Cook for 4–5 minutes until golden. Carefully turn the fillets over and cook the flesh side for a further 1–2 minutes until cooked through.

Serve the radish slaw on a plate, add the Szechuan onion and lay the sea bream on top. Scatter with the mint tips.

Serves: 4
Preparation time: 15 minutes
Cooking time: about 20 minutes

3 tbsp vegetable oil
1 onion, finely sliced
6 Szechuan peppercorns, finely crushed
2 tbsp sweet sherry
2 tbsp toasted sesame oil
2 tbsp soy sauce
50g unsalted peanuts, roasted and finely chopped
4 skin-on, pin-boned sea bream fillets
sea salt and freshly ground black pepper
mint tips, to serve

FOR THE RADISH SLAW
2 tbsp sesame oil
1 tsp rice wine vinegar
1 tbsp finely chopped coriander
1 tbsp pickled ginger, finely sliced
2 watermelon radishes, peeled and finely sliced into rounds

This is a simple but very tasty dish. If you are not a fan of artichokes, substitute green beans, or try tinned white beans for a hearty supper. You can use fresh artichokes, but they are a huge amount of work to prepare and top-quality jarred artichoke hearts work just as well.

PAN-FRIED POLLOCK WITH CAPERS, ARTICHOKES AND BROWN BUTTER

Heat the oil in a large non-stick frying pan over high heat. Season the pollock fillets with sea salt and carefully place them in the pan, skin side down. Cook for 4 minutes until the skin is golden, then carefully turn them over and cook for a further 2 minutes until browned. When the other side is browned, add half of the butter. When the butter starts to foam, spoon it over the fish repeatedly for a further 1–2 minutes until the fish is cooked through. Gently remove the fish from the pan and set aside on a plate somewhere warm.

Place the pan back on medium-high heat and add the remaining butter. Keep the pan moving until the butter is a nutty brown colour. Add the lemon zest and juice and cook for 2 minutes, then add the capers and artichoke hearts and some black pepper and warm through. Stir through half the rocket and parsley.

Place the fish in four deep bowls, then spoon the artichoke hearts over and around the fish and scatter with the remaining rocket and parsley.

Serves: 4
Preparation time: 5 minutes
Cooking time: around 10 minutes

2 tbsp vegetable oil
4 boneless pollock fillets, skin on and scored (150–180g each)
50g butter, diced
grated zest and juice of ½ lemon
2 tbsp capers, chopped
8 artichoke hearts in oil, drained and quartered
70g wild rocket
1 tbsp chopped flat-leaf parsley
sea salt and freshly ground black pepper

Baking sea bass whole is one of the best ways to eat it. To avoid getting a mouthful of bones, be careful when removing the flesh. It is a matter of almost peeling it away from the bone, rather than forcing it in any way. Once one fillet is off, take the tail end in your hand and just pull: the bones will come off the flesh very easily.

BAKED SEA BASS WITH SESAME AND LEMONGRASS

Preheat the oven to 180°C/160°C fan/gas 4 and line a roasting dish with baking parchment.

Gently score lines in the skin on each side of the sea bass, approximately 1.5cm apart. Place the bass in the lined roasting dish.

Finely grate the lemongrass stalks and ginger into a bowl. Add the sesame oil, lime zest and juice, fish sauce and miso paste and whisk together.

Pour a third of the lemongrass dressing on one side of the bass and rub it into the skin. Turn the bass over and repeat on the other side with another third of the dressing.

Place the lime quarters in the roasting dish with the sea bass and bake in the oven for about 25 minutes, until the flesh in the centre of the fish is cooked through – gently pull it away from the middle of the fish, near the bone, and check it's cooked through and not opaque. Place the sesame seeds on a baking tray underneath the fish for the final 6–8 minutes and toast until golden.

Transfer the fish and lime wedges to a large serving platter and drizzle the tahini over the top of the bass. Drizzle with the remaining lemongrass dressing and finish with the toasted sesame seeds.

Serves: 4
Preparation time: 15 minutes
Cooking time: 25 minutes

1 whole sea bass, gutted and scaled
(1.2–1.5kg)
4 lemongrass stalks
2cm piece of fresh ginger, peeled
50ml toasted sesame oil
grated zest and juice of 1 lime, plus
1 lime, quartered
2 tbsp fish sauce
1 tbsp white miso paste
1½ tbsp white sesame seeds
2 tbsp tahini

Salmon is a great fish to cook at home as its natural oils mean it's always succulent and here is my fresher version of the classic pairing with mayonnaise. Buy skinless fillets if you prefer, but if you choose to leave the skin on, the secret for crispy skin is a hot, non-stick pan, which allows the skin to slowly crisp up. When the salmon goes in the pan, put it in skin side down and do not move it until the skin begins to brown at the edges – this way it will not stick.

SALMON WITH BEETROOT AIOLI AND WATERCRESS SALAD

Pour the beetroot juice into a medium saucepan over medium heat. Bring to the boil, then reduce the heat and simmer for 10–12 minutes until the liquid has reduced to about 2 tablespoons of syrup. Take care to ensure it does not burn though, as it will lose its vibrant purple colour. Remove from the heat and leave to cool.

To make the aioli, put the egg yolks in a bowl and, while whisking continuously with a balloon whisk, add the vinegar, garlic and Dijon mustard. Put both oils in a jug and slowly drizzle into the egg yolk mixture, whisking constantly as you do so. When it has reached a very thick mayonnaise consistency, whisk in the beetroot syrup. Season to taste with sea salt.

To cook the salmon, heat the vegetable oil in a large non-stick frying pan over high heat. When hot, season the salmon on both sides with sea salt then add them to the pan and cook, skin side down, for 4–5 minutes. When the skin is crisp, carefully turn the salmon over and cook the flesh side. Depending on the thickness of the salmon, cook for a further 4–6 minutes, until crisp on the outside and just cooked in the middle. Remove from the heat, transfer the fish to a plate and allow the fillets to rest for a couple of minutes.

To make the watercress salad, whisk the oil and lemon juice together in a bowl. Mix with the watercress and season well with sea salt and pepper.

Serve the salmon fillets with a good spoonful of aioli and the dressed watercress.

Serves: 4
Preparation time: 15 minutes
Cooking time: 10 minutes

2 tbsp vegetable oil
4 portions of salmon fillet, skin on, pin-boned, skin scored (about 170g each)
sea salt and freshly ground black pepper

FOR THE BEETROOT AIOLI
250ml beetroot juice
3 egg yolks
1 tsp white wine vinegar
1 garlic clove, finely grated
½ tsp Dijon mustard
150ml groundnut oil
150ml light olive oil

FOR THE WATERCRESS SALAD
2 tbsp extra virgin olive oil
1 tsp lemon juice
1 large bunch of watercress (about 80g), leaves picked and stalks finely chopped

Kimchi is a traditional Korean dish of fermented cabbage and spice which I find works really well as an accompaniment, particularly to fish. The longer you leave it the more tangy it becomes (make it at least 2 days before serving). It can be kept in the fridge for up to 3 months.

SALT-AND-PEPPER PLAICE WITH KIMCHI

To make the kimchi, place all the ingredients, apart from the cabbage, in a blender and blend to form a paste. Transfer to a bowl with the cabbage and, using gloves, massage the paste into it for 5 minutes. Pack into a jar, seal with a lid and leave somewhere cool for a minimum of 48 hours.

If you are scattering with chilli, prepare it now. Heat 1 tablespoon of the vegetable oil in a frying pan over medium-high heat. When hot, add the red chilli and cook for 1 minute until crisp, then transfer to a bowl.

Pour enough vegetable oil in a deep-fat fryer or large, deep saucepan to come up to 6cm and heat it to 160°C.

To prepare the seasoned flour, crush or mill the peppercorns then mix them in a bowl with the table salt and potato flour.

Sprinkle the plaice strips with the rock salt and leave for 5 minutes. Rinse off the salt thoroughly under cold running water and pat the fish dry with kitchen paper.

Liberally coat the plaice strips in the seasoned flour then carefully drop them into the hot oil and fry for 5–6 minutes until deep golden and crisp (fry them in batches). Carefully take the goujons out of the pan or fryer with a large slotted spoon and place on kitchen paper to absorb the excess oil.

Serve with the kimchi and sour cream or crème fraîche (if you wish).

Serves: 4
Preparation time: 20 minutes, plus
    48 hours fermenting
Cooking time: 5 minutes

vegetable oil, for frying and deep-frying
1 red chilli, finely sliced (optional)
4 skinless plaice fillets (approx. 400g in
    total), sliced into finger-width strips
approx. 4 tbsp rock salt
4 tbsp sour cream or crème fraîche
    (optional)

FOR THE KIMCHI
2 garlic cloves, peeled
4cm piece of fresh ginger, peeled and
    finely grated
15g palm sugar, finely grated
3 tbsp fish sauce
15g Korean red pepper powder
    (or gochujang, if unavailable)
3 tbsp rice wine vinegar
1 tsp table salt
1 Chinese cabbage, finely chopped

FOR THE SEASONED FLOUR
½ tsp Szechuan peppercorns
½ tsp whole black peppercorns
½ tsp table salt
80g potato flour

This dish focuses on two key Japanese ingredients: miso and nori. Most of us know nori as the green seaweed that surrounds sushi rolls, but it is in fact very versatile and can be used in sauces or salads, too. Given it is highly susceptible to moisture, use dry scissors when cutting it. Boulangère potatoes are rather moreish, so don't be afraid to make more than you need.

ROASTED POLLOCK WITH MISO BUTTER, NORI AND BOULANGÈRE POTATOES

Preheat the oven to 200°C/180°C fan/gas 6 and line a 20cm square cake tin with baking parchment.

Put 1 tablespoon of the miso paste in a large bowl. Melt 150g of the butter and whisk it into the miso until combined.

Put the sliced potatoes in the large bowl with the miso and melted butter. Use your hands to coat the slices all over. Put half of the fine nori strips in the bowl with the potatoes and mix to combine. Layer the potatoes in the bottom of the lined cake tin and keep layering, evenly, until you have used all of the potatoes. Cover the tin with foil and bake for 15 minutes. Remove the foil and bake for a further 10 minutes. Remove and chill in the fridge until cold. When cold, remove the potato from the tin and cut it into eight rectangles.

Heat 4 tablespoons of the oil in a large non-stick frying pan over medium heat. When hot, carefully add the pieces of the boulangère potatoes and fry for about 5 minutes, turning them until golden all over. (You might have to do this in batches.) Add some of the remaining butter to the pan and, once melted, spoon it over the boulangère potatoes. Remove from the heat and keep warm while you cook the fish.

Whisk the remaining tablespoon of miso paste in a bowl with the remaining soft butter until smooth.

For the fish, heat the remaining vegetable oil in a large non-stick frying pan over high heat. When hot, season the fish fillets on both sides then carefully place them in the pan and cook them for 3 minutes on each side, until golden (fry them in batches, if necessary, to avoid overcrowding the pan). Add the miso butter and the vegetable stock (with all the fillets back in the pan, if you

Serves: 4

Preparation time: 20 minutes, plus chilling

Cooking time: 40–50 minutes

2 tbsp white miso paste

200g soft butter

6 medium King Edward or other floury potatoes, peeled and finely sliced into 2mm-thick rounds

1 sheet nori, cut with scissors into fine strips

6 tbsp vegetable oil

4 skinless pollock or cod fillets (140–180g each)

100ml Vegetable Stock (page 57)

1 tbsp finely chopped coriander

sea salt and freshly ground black pepper

were frying them in batches), as well as the remaining shredded nori, and turn down the heat. Cover the fish with a circle of baking parchment and fry for a further minute until cooked through.

To serve, place two pieces of the boulangere potato on each plate with the fish beside it. Spoon over the sauce from the frying pan, scatter over the coriander and serve.

Freshly hot-smoked salmon has an unbeatable flavour and texture. Orzo is an underused pasta – it cooks very quickly and is also perfect in salads. If you are not familiar with it, it is rice-shaped and very versatile. Don't skimp on the dill in this recipe as the vibrant savouriness it adds is delicious.

HOT SMOKED SALMON, ORZO, CRÈME FRAÎCHE AND DILL SALAD

Preheat the oven to 110°C/90°C fan/gas ¼.

Combine the rock salt and demerara sugar and liberally coat the salmon portions in the mixture (on all sides). Leave to cure for 10 minutes, then rinse the salmon thoroughly under cold running water and pat dry with kitchen paper.

Smoke the fish according to the method on page 165. When you see smoke, seal the tin and transfer to the oven for 8–12 minutes, depending on how thick your salmon fillets are. Remove the tray from the oven and leave to rest for 5 minutes before you remove the foil. Flake the smoked salmon into large chunks and set aside.

To make the crème fraîche dressing, place all the ingredients in a bowl and mix together. Season to taste.

Cook the orzo pasta according to the packet instructions. Drain well, tip it into a bowl, add the extra virgin olive oil and spinach leaves and toss.

To serve, divide the orzo and spinach between four plates and spoon the crème fraîche dressing on top. Finish with the flaked, smoked salmon and an extra grind of pepper to serve.

Serves: 4
Preparation time: 15 minutes, plus
    10 minutes curing
Cooking time: around 20 minutes,
    plus 20 minutes smoking

2 tbsp rock salt
2 tbsp demerara sugar
4 skinless and pin-boned salmon
    fillet portions (about 140g each)
1 x quantity of Smoke Mix (page 165),
    using 25g chamomile tea leaves
300g orzo pasta
1 tbsp extra virgin olive oil
100g baby spinach leaves, washed

FOR THE CRÈME FRAÎCHE
DRESSING
100g crème fraîche
1 tbsp good-quality mayonnaise
1 tbsp white wine vinegar
2 tbsp capers in brine, strained and
    finely chopped
2 gherkins, finely chopped
2 tbsp finely chopped dill
grated zest of ½ lemon, plus a small
    squeeze of juice
sea salt and freshly ground black
    pepper

Cooking mussels in an already flavoursome stock not only ensures they are tasty but creates a delicious broth which can be eaten like a soup. I have added samphire, which has become widely available in the past couple of years and enhances any seafood dish (not surprising given it tastes of the ocean!).

MOULES MARINIÈRE

Rinse the mussels well in a colander under cold running water to remove any grit. Remove any visible barnacles and dirt. Pull any beards towards the hinged end of the mussel shell and pull firmly until they come out. If any of the mussels are open, tap them hard against a work surface and if they don't close, discard them.

Melt 50g of the butter in a large saucepan big enough to fit all of the mussels (with a lid) over medium heat. Add the shallots and bay leaves and cook for 5–7 minutes until the shallots are soft but not browned, then add the wine, cider and table salt. Bring to the boil and simmer for 10 minutes, then add the stock. Simmer for a further 5 minutes then add the cleaned mussels, cover with the lid and cook over high heat for 4 minutes. Remove the lid and check that most of the mussels have opened – if quite a few are still closed, replace the lid and cook for a further minute. Strain the liquor into a medium saucepan and keep the mussels hot in the large saucepan covered with the lid. Discard any unopened mussels.

Bring the liquor to the boil and gradually whisk in the remaining 50g of butter, cube by cube, until you have a thickened and flavoursome sauce. Add the samphire and simmer for 2 minutes, then stir in the chopped tarragon. Season to taste with sea salt and pepper.

Divide the mussels between four large bowls and spoon over the sauce. Serve with crusty bread.

Serves: 4
Preparation time: 25 minutes
Cooking time: around 30 minutes

2kg mussels
100g unsalted butter, diced
4 shallots, finely sliced
2 bay leaves
150ml white wine
150ml dry cider
½ tsp table salt
150ml Chicken or Vegetable Stock
    (pages 83 and 57)
100g samphire
¼ bunch of tarragon, leaves chopped
sea salt and freshly ground black
    pepper
crusty bread, to serve

Unless it is cooked slowly at a low temperature, all squid needs is a quick flash in a hot pan – any longer in a pan and it becomes rubbery and unpleasant to eat. Freezing squid also tenderises it, so it is a great thing to have on standby at home.

CHARGRILLED SQUID WITH COURGETTES, WHITE BEANS AND LEMON DRESSING

Combine the ingredients for the lemon dressing and mix well. Season with sea salt and pepper.

Open up the squid tubes by cutting them down one side. Lay the squid out flat and, with the tip of the knife, carefully score diagonal lines along the squid in one direction and then the other, at an equal distance from each other, to create diamonds. Slice across the scored squid to create 1cm-wide strips then put it in a shallow dish with half of the lemon dressing. Leave to marinate for 10 minutes.

Heat a grill pan over high heat until smoking. Drizzle the courgette slices with the vegetable oil, season them with sea salt and pepper and grill, in batches, for 2–3 minutes on each side. Put the grilled courgettes in a bowl.

Grill the marinated squid in batches, so the grill pan stays hot, just for 1–2 minutes until lightly coloured and firm. Remove the squid from the pan, transfer to a plate and add a splash of olive oil. Add the beans and shallots to the grill pan and heat through. When hot, place the beans in the bowl with the courgettes and toss with the herbs and remaining dressing, top with the squid and serve.

Serves: 4
Preparation time: 15 minutes
Cooking time: about 15 minutes

600g squid tubes, cleaned
2 courgettes, cut into 5mm-thick
    diagonal slices
2 tbsp vegetable oil
1 x 400g tin cannellini beans, drained
2 shallots, finely diced
2 tbsp chopped flat-leaf parsley
2 tbsp chopped tarragon
sea salt and freshly ground black
    pepper
lemon wedges, to serve

FOR THE LEMON DRESSING
grated zest and juice of 2 lemons
4 tbsp extra virgin olive oil, plus extra
    for drizzling
1 garlic clove, finely grated
½ tsp fennel seeds, toasted and finely
    crushed

Freshly cooked lobster is hard to beat. Being such a luxury item it is important not to overcook it, as it will end up rubbery and chalky. Always purchase lobsters raw as you can then control how they are cooked, and how long for, so you're not disappointed with the end result. Späetzle is a small, pasta-like dumpling that is simple to make and goes perfectly with the lobster. Yuzu is a citrus fruit prized for its aromatic and perfumed flavour, and can be found in some supermarkets and specialist shops. *See image on following pages.*

LOBSTER WITH YUZU EMULSION, SAFFRON SPÄETZLE AND FRESH PEAS

To make the späetzle, put the saffron in the milk in a medium bowl and set aside to infuse for 10 minutes. Whisk in the eggs, then add the flour. Whisk well and add a pinch of sea salt. Bring a large pan of salted water to the boil and press the späetzle dough through a colander into the boiling water. When the späetzle rise to the top (this should take about 1 minute), remove them with a slotted spoon and place them in a bowl of cold water to stop them cooking. Drain and set aside.

Place the lobsters in the freezer for 30 minutes.

To make the yuzu emulsion, heat the stock in a saucepan. When hot, whisk in the butter, a cube at a time, until emulsified. Add the yuzu juice and season to taste.

Preheat the grill on your oven to its highest setting.

Take one lobster and twist off the claws and legs. With a large knife, cut the lobster in half lengthways, and wash well under cold running water. Pat dry with kitchen paper then place the pieces of lobster in a roasting dish, flesh side up.

Serves: 4
Preparation time: 40 minutes, plus freezing
Cooking time: around 15 minutes

2 live lobsters
40g butter
2 sprigs of thyme, leaves picked
grated zest and juice of ½ lemon
150g sugar snap peas
100g fresh podded peas
1 tbsp chopped tarragon
sea salt and freshly ground black pepper
pea shoots, to serve

Using the back of a knife, or a lobster cracker, crack the claws open and remove the meat. Place the meat, with the legs, under the lobster halves. Repeat with the second lobster.

Melt the butter in a pan and add the thyme leaves, lemon zest and juice. Season well with sea salt then pour the butter over the lobster flesh.

Melt the butter for the späetzle in a large frying pan. When hot, add the späetzle and cook for 3–5 minutes until golden.

Heat the emulsion, add the sugar snap peas and fresh peas and cook until tender. Just before serving, finish with the tarragon.

Put the dish of lobsters in the oven on a shelf halfway up from the bottom (about 20cm from the grill). Grill for 6–10 minutes until golden and just cooked through.

Spoon the späetzle onto plates, add the yuzu and pea emulsions and top each serving with half a lobster. Drizzle the butter and cooking juices from the lobster over the top, scatter over the pea shoots and serve.

FOR THE SPÄETZLE
pinch of saffron strands
3 tbsp milk, warmed
3 eggs
180g plain flour
40g butter

FOR THE YUZU EMULSION
150ml Chicken or Vegetable Stock
  (pages 83 and 57)
50g butter, diced
30ml yuzu juice (or more to taste)

FROM THE STORECUPBOARD

Apricot, almond and Earl Grey are a great trio to put together. If you are making this tart out of season then I would suggest using good-quality tinned apricots. Alternatively, substitute any other stone fruit – plums are a good alternative in the colder months.

APRICOT, ALMOND AND EARL GREY TART

To make the pastry, rub together the flour, sea salt, cold butter and sugar in a bowl (or blitz in a food processor) until you have a breadcrumb-like texture. Gradually add the beaten egg to form a soft, pliable dough. Wrap the dough in clingfilm and chill for 30 minutes.

Roll out the pastry on a lightly floured surface and use it to line a 23cm loose-bottomed tart tin, leaving a little excess pastry to hang over the edges. Return to the fridge for 20 minutes.

Meanwhile, preheat the oven to 220°C/200°C fan/gas 7.

Line the pastry case with baking parchment and fill with baking beans. Sit the tart case on a baking sheet and bake for 5 minutes. Reduce the oven temperature to 180°C/160°C fan/gas 4 and bake the tart case for a further 15 minutes, until it starts to turn golden and become firm. Remove the baking beans and parchment, brush with the egg yolk and return the case to the oven for a further 5 minutes, until evenly golden. Remove from the oven and allow to cool slightly. When cool enough to handle, trim away the excess pastry with a sharp knife.

To make the frangipane, beat together the sugar and butter in a bowl until light and creamy. Add the eggs one at a time, beating well after each addition. Finally, mix in the pinch of salt and almonds.

Spread 3 tablespoons of the apricot jam on the bottom of the pastry case followed by the frangipane, then arrange the sliced apricots on top, in a circular formation, to cover the whole tart. Bake for 40–45 minutes, until deep golden and the frangipane has just set in the centre. Remove from the oven and leave to cool on a wire rack for at least 15 minutes.

Serves: 10–12
Preparation time: 30 minutes, plus 50 minutes chilling
Cooking time: 1 hour 10 minutes, plus cooling

FOR THE PASTRY
175g plain flour, plus extra for dusting
pinch of sea salt
115g cold butter, diced
50g caster sugar
1 egg, beaten, plus 1 egg yolk

FOR THE FRANGIPANE
150g caster sugar
150g soft butter
3 eggs
pinch of sea salt
185g ground almonds

4 tbsp apricot jam
5–7 large, ripe apricots, stones removed and each sliced into 8
3 tsp Earl Grey tea leaves or 1 tea bag
1 tbsp Amaretto or other almond liqueur

While the tart is cooling, bring 50ml water to the boil then add the tea leaves or tea bag. Remove from the heat and allow to infuse for 6 minutes then strain. Mix the tea in a bowl with the remaining tablespoon of apricot jam and the Amaretto or almond liqueur. Liberally brush the top of the tart a few times with this syrup (you might have some left over). Leave to cool completely in the tin before removing, slicing and serving.

I am a big fan of chocolate and orange and this is a great dessert that incorporates the two flavours. You can substitute the orange for other citrus flavours such as lime, lemon or grapefruit. Do try the Negroni cream, too, as adding a cocktail to a dessert can only be a good thing.

DARK CHOCOLATE ORANGE TARTS WITH NEGRONI CREAM

To make the chocolate pastry, beat the butter and icing sugar in a bowl with an electric whisk or in the bowl of a standmixer until light and creamy. Weigh the beaten egg then gradually add half of it to the butter and sugar (discard the rest). Once smooth, add the flour, cocoa powder and salt, and mix together until combined. Form into a square then wrap it in clingfilm and chill for 30 minutes.

Preheat the oven to 200°C/180°C fan/gas 6 and line a baking tray with baking parchment.

Roll out the pastry and cut it into four 7cm circles using a pastry cutter. Place the pastry circles on the lined baking tray and chill for 20 minutes. Once chilled, bake for about 10 minutes, until the pastry is cooked through. Remove from the oven and leave to cool.

To make the chocolate orange filling, put the milk, cream and orange zest in a medium saucepan and bring to the boil, stirring frequently.

Put the egg yolks and caster sugar in a heatproof bowl and whisk to combine. Slowly pour in the hot milk mixture, whisking continuously. Return the mixture back to the pan and cook over very low heat for 5–7 minutes, stirring constantly, until the mixture coats the back of a wooden spoon.

Put the chopped chocolate in a large heatproof bowl. Strain the hot milk mixture through a fine sieve onto the chocolate. Cover the bowl with clingfilm and allow to sit for 5 minutes, then remove the clingfilm and whisk until smooth.

Serves: 4 very generously
Preparation time: 30 minutes, plus 50 minutes chilling
Cooking time: around 10 minutes, plus 2 hours chilling

FOR THE CHOCOLATE PASTRY
20g soft butter, diced
60g icing sugar
1 egg, beaten
65g plain flour
5g cocoa powder
pinch of salt

FOR THE CHOCOLATE ORANGE FILLING
80ml milk
200ml whipping cream
grated zest of 1 orange
4 egg yolks
40g caster sugar
220g dark chocolate (minimum 70% cocoa solids), chopped

Line four muffin holes of a muffin tin (7cm in diameter and 3cm deep) with a double layer of clingfilm. Spoon the chocolate-orange mixture into the holes, leave to cool slightly, then top with a pastry disc. Transfer to the fridge and leave for at least 2 hours to set.

To make the negroni cream, lightly whisk the double cream in a bowl until soft peaks form. Add the gin, vermouth and Campari and whisk again until the cream forms stiff peaks.

To serve, lift out the tarts with the help of the clingfilm. Use a hot palette knife to smooth over the chocolate for a clean finish. Serve with the negroni cream.

FOR THE NEGRONI CREAM
100ml double cream
1 tsp gin, or to taste
1 tsp dark vermouth, or to taste
1 tsp Campari, or to taste

When trying to think how I could improve upon a classic egg custard tart, the thought that sprang to mind was to enhance the flavour in a caramel-like way. I decided to use dark brown sugar and the result is a lovely change from the classic! It makes a delicious pudding, served with crème fraîche. But I am also partial to it with a cup of tea in the afternoon.

BROWN SUGAR TART

To make the pastry, rub together the flour, cinnamon, sea salt, sugar and cold butter in a bowl (or blitz in a food processor) until you have a breadcrumb-like texture. Gradually add the beaten egg to form a soft, pliable dough. Wrap the dough in clingfilm and chill for 30 minutes.

Roll out the pastry on a lightly floured surface and use it to line a 23cm loose-bottomed tart tin (at least 3cm deep), leaving a little excess pastry to hang over the edges. Return to the fridge for 20 minutes.

Meanwhile, preheat the oven to 220°C/200°C fan/gas 7.

Line the pastry case with baking parchment and fill with baking beans. Sit the tart case on a baking sheet and bake for 5 minutes. Reduce the oven temperature to 180°C/160°C fan/gas 4 and bake for a further 15 minutes, until the pastry starts to turn golden and become firm. Remove the baking beans and parchment, brush with the egg yolk and return the case to the oven for a further 5 minutes, until evenly golden. Remove from the oven and allow to cool slightly. When cool enough to handle, trim away the excess pastry with a sharp knife. Reduce the oven temperature to 150°C/130°C fan/gas 2.

To make the custard, pour both creams into a saucepan and bring to the boil.

Serves: 10–12
Preparation time: 35 minutes, plus
    50 minutes chilling
Cooking time: 1 hour 5 minutes, plus
    2 hours cooling

4 tbsp caster sugar, for bruléeing

FOR THE PASTRY
175g plain flour, plus extra for dusting
½ tsp ground cinnamon
pinch of sea salt
50g caster sugar
115g cold butter, diced
1 egg, beaten, plus 1 egg yolk

Meanwhile, whisk the egg yolks and dark brown sugar together in a heatproof bowl.

Remove the pan from the heat as soon as the cream reaches boiling point and pour the hot cream mix into the yolk mix, whisking continuously, until the sugar has dissolved. Strain through a fine sieve into a jug and skim away any froth on top of the mix.

Place the tart case back in the oven for 5 minutes then, while it is still in the oven, open the oven door and carefully pour in the hot custard (you may not need all the custard).

Gently close the oven door and bake the tart for 30 minutes. Open the oven door and gently nudge the tart – if it is still rather wobbly, bake for a few more minutes, then check again. It is ready when the filling wobbles just very slightly in the centre of the tart. Carefully remove from the oven and leave to cool fully, for at least 2 hours, in the tin before removing it.

Slice the tart then dust each piece with a little sugar. Blowtorch the top to caramelise the sugar.

FOR THE CUSTARD
300ml whipping cream
300ml double cream
11 egg yolks
90g soft dark brown sugar

This is a great dish to make in the height of summer, when peaches are at their best. You can use nectarines instead of peaches, if you prefer. The ricotta adds a lovely savouriness to the dish and balances out some of the sweetness.

POACHED PEACHES WITH OAT CRUMB AND RICOTTA

To make the poached peaches, put the honey, sugar, white wine, saffron, peppercorns, bay leaves, lemon juice and peel in a large saucepan. Top up with 400ml water and bring to the boil. Reduce to a very gentle simmer and add the peaches. Cover with a lid, or a circle of baking parchment that fits inside the pan, and cook for 25–35 minutes until the peaches are soft and the skin peels away easily.

Remove the peaches from the cooking liquor using a slotted spoon and place them on a tray to cool. When cool enough to handle, gently peel off the skin.

Place the cooking liquor over high heat and let it reduce by two-thirds, until you have a thick syrup. Strain it through a sieve into a bowl or jug and leave to cool.

To make the oat crumb, preheat the oven to 210°C/190°C fan/gas 7 and line a baking tray with baking parchment. Mix the flour, sugar and oats together in a bowl then, using your fingertips, rub the soft butter into the mixture. Tip it out onto the lined baking tray, spread it out in an even layer and bake for 12–15 minutes until golden, stirring regularly. Remove from the oven and leave to cool.

Whisk the ricotta in a bowl with the lemon zest and liqueur (if using).

To serve, cut the poached peach quarters in half again. Coat them in the syrup and place in a large bowl or divide between four small bowls. Dot or pipe the ricotta over the peaches, break up the oat crumb and scatter it on top.

Serves: 4
Preparation time: 20 minutes
Cooking time: 45 minutes, plus cooling

120g ricotta cheese
grated zest of 1 lemon
1 tbsp peach schnapps or peach liqueur (optional)

FOR THE POACHED PEACHES
100g honey
100g caster sugar
100ml white wine
pinch of saffron
4 whole white peppercorns
2 bay leaves
juice and pared peel of 1 lemon
4 large ripe peaches, quartered and stones removed

FOR THE OAT CRUMB
50g plain flour
50g caster sugar
50g rolled oats
50g soft butter

My version of a dinner party classic that looks, and tastes, rather wonderful. Fresh figs are such a treat and this is a great dessert that enhances their perfume-like quality. They pair extremely well with ginger and the little kick of ginger wine just enhances the flavour of the cheesecake even more.

FIG AND GINGER CHEESECAKE

Put the ginger biscuits and diced stem ginger in a food processor and pulse until the mixture forms small crumbs. Add the melted butter and blend until combined. Press into the bottom of a 23cm springform cake tin and chill.

Soak the gelatine leaves in a bowl of cold water for 5 minutes.

Beat the cream cheese in a bowl until smooth. Add the crème fraîche and whisk until combined.

Heat the ginger wine in a small pan over low heat. Squeeze the excess water from the gelatine and stir it into the hot ginger wine until completely dissolved. Remove from the heat and leave to cool slightly for a few minutes, then stir in the syrup from the stem ginger jar. Whisk it into the cream cheese mix until smooth, then sift over the icing sugar and whisk that in too. Lightly whisk the double cream in a bowl until it forms soft peaks then gently fold into the cream cheese mix.

Spoon the cream onto the chilled ginger biscuit base and smooth the surface using a hot palette knife. Chill for at least 2–3 hours until set.

Cut the figs into 5mm slices and place them on top of the cheesecake, overlapping them in a circular formation. Mix the apricot jam in a cup with 2 tablespoons of boiling water to make a glaze then gently brush the glaze over the figs. Chill for another 20 minutes, then slice and serve.

Serves: 10–12
Preparation time: 40 minutes, plus
    2–3 hours chilling

200g ginger biscuits
100g stem ginger in syrup, finely
    diced, plus 6 tbsp syrup
100g butter, melted
3 gelatine leaves
300g full-fat cream cheese
200g crème fraîche
50ml ginger wine
60g icing sugar
125ml double cream
5 ripe figs
2 tbsp apricot jam

Strawberries and cream is a classic combination that works so well. To take it a step further, I've added a more savoury element to it by cold-smoking the mascarpone. It gives the dish an extra dimension and works so well with fresh, perfectly ripe strawberries. Always serve strawberries at room temperature as they will have much more flavour.

STRAWBERRIES, SMOKED MASCARPONE AND SHORTBREAD

Smoke the mascarpone according to the method on page 165, spreading it as thinly as possible in a foil dish, and put the dish on the smoking rack. Once smoked, remove the tray and set aside for 10 minutes. Remove the foil then scrape the smoked mascarpone into a bowl and whisk to loosen it. Cover and chill until ready to serve.

Preheat the oven to 200°C/180°C fan/gas 6 and line a baking tray with baking parchment.

To make the shortbread, put all of the dry ingredients into a food processor and blitz to combine. Add the butter and lemon zest and pulse in short bursts until you have a dough that clumps together in little bits. It may take some time for the butter to work into the dry ingredients. Tip onto the lined tray and spread it out evenly. Bake for 10–15 minutes until golden and crispy, turning the tray regularly in the oven to ensure it cooks evenly. Remove from the oven and leave to cool.

Remove the stalks from the strawberries and cut any larger ones in half or quarters. Toss them in the strawberry liqueur and divide them between six bowls. Sprinkle generously with the shortbread crumb then add a spoon of smoked mascarpone on top to serve.

Serves: 6
Preparation time: 20 minutes
Cooking time: 15 minutes, plus
    cooling

1 x quantity of Smoke Mix (page 165),
    using 1 tbsp black tea leaves
200g mascarpone
600g strawberries
6 tbsp strawberry liqueur, Cointreau
    or crème de cassis

FOR THE SHORTBREAD CRUMB
60g plain flour
35g cornflour
35g icing sugar, sifted
pinch of sea salt
60g cold diced butter
grated zest of ½ lemon

Buttery pastry paired with nuts and spices is always a good combination. I have added a slight twist on classic baklava here with the addition of rhubarb and burnt honey. Be warned – it is rather moreish!

RHUBARB BAKLAVA WITH BURNT HONEY

Preheat the oven to 190°C/170°C fan/gas 5 and line a 20 x 30cm baking dish with greaseproof paper.

Melt the butter. Lay one half of a sheet of filo pastry in the bottom of the baking dish and brush it liberally with melted butter. Repeat with 5 more half sheets of pastry.

Put the rhubarb, caster sugar, chopped nuts and ground cardamom in a large bowl and mix until combined. Spread the mixture over the filo pastry base.

Cover the rhubarb and nut mix with another layer of filo pastry and brush liberally with melted butter. Repeat with the remaining 5 sheets.

Score the top of the pastry with a crisscross pattern then place in the oven for 45–55 minutes until golden. Remove from the oven and set aside.

Place the honey in a medium saucepan over high heat. Boil the honey until it begins to colour to a deep golden. Carefully – it will bubble – add the orange blossom water and remove the pan from the heat. Mix well then pour the honey liberally over the top of the baklava and leave to cool. Once it's completely cool, slice it into 20 pieces with a serrated knife.

Makes: around 20 pieces
Preparation time: 25 minutes
Cooking time: 55 minutes, plus
    cooling

100g butter, plus extra for greasing
1 x 270g pack filo pastry (6 sheets),
    cut in half widthways (they should
    be roughly 19 x 26cm once cut)
200g rhubarb, cut into 5mm dice
4 tbsp caster sugar
100g pistachio nuts, roughly chopped
100g walnuts, roughly chopped
1 tsp ground cardamom
200g runny honey
a dash of orange blossom water
    (or to taste)

For a lighter end to a meal, try this refreshing dessert. The mint, lime and chamomile add a new twist to a classic fruit salad. As always, ensure the fruit you use is ripe and at room temperature to serve, as the flavour is duller on your palate when produce is cold.

STONE FRUIT SALAD WITH CHAMOMILE AND LIME GRANITA

To make the chamomile and lime granita, put 100ml of water in a small saucepan, bring to the boil and add the chamomile tea and sugar. Remove from the heat, cover and allow to infuse for 5 minutes. Strain through a fine sieve into a clean bowl. Add the lime juice, pour the mixture into a small shallow metal tray or cake tin (not one with a removable base) and transfer to the freezer for 1 hour.

Use a fork to scrape the mixture then return it to the freezer, repeating the scraping process a couple of times, once an hour, until you have fluffy ice crystals.

When the granita has fully frozen, assemble the fruit salad.

Halve the stone fruit and slice them. Arrange on a platter and grate the zest from the lime over the top. Finely slice the mint leaves and scatter them on top. Remove the granita from the freezer, give it a final scrape with a fork, then spoon it on top of the fruit.

Serves: 4
Preparation time: 15 minutes, plus freezing

FOR THE CHAMOMILE AND LIME GRANITA
2 tsp chamomile tea leaves or 2 chamomile tea bags
50g caster sugar
50ml fresh lime juice (from 2–3 limes)

FOR THE STONE FRUIT SALAD
2 ripe apricots
1 ripe peach
1 ripe nectarine
100g cherries
1 lime
6 mint leaves

Gooseberries have such a great, aromatic flavour. Given they are rather sour, they do need quite a lot of sweetness added but it also means they have enough acidity in them to set a posset. When making possets, remember to simmer the cream for long enough, otherwise they will not set.

GOOSEBERRY POSSET WITH ROSEMARY AND ALMOND CAKES

Place the gooseberries in a medium saucepan and add 50ml water. Place over medium heat and simmer for 10–15 minutes until soft. Allow to cool slightly then place in a blender or food processor and blend until smooth. If you're using tinned gooseberries, just purée them with the 50ml water, without cooking them.

Add the cream and sugar to a medium saucepan and place over medium heat. Bring to the boil and simmer for 6 minutes, stirring frequently. Remove from the heat then whisk in the gooseberry purée. Pass through a fine sieve into a jug, pour into 6 glasses or ramekins and chill for at least 3–4 hours, until firm.

To make the cakes, mix the ground almonds, rosemary and flour together in a medium bowl. Add the caster sugar and egg whites and whisk together to combine.

Melt the butter in a small saucepan over high heat. Reduce the heat to medium and cook until it becomes a golden, nutty brown colour. Slowly pour this into the almond mixture, mixing as you pour. Cover and chill in the fridge for 30 minutes.

Preheat the oven to 200°C/180°C fan/gas 6 and lightly grease a 12-hole non-stick bun tin or fairy-cake tin with oil.

Divide the cake mixture between the holes and bake for 15 minutes until lightly golden and just firm to the touch. Remove them from the tin immediately.

Garnish the possets with the gooseberries. Sprinkle over the rosemary and serve with the warm rosemary and almond cakes.

Serves: 6
Preparation time: 25 minutes, plus
    3 hours chilling
Cooking time: 20–30 minutes

200g gooseberries, fresh or frozen
    (or 145g tinned, drained and
    rinsed)
600ml double cream
190g caster sugar
50g gooseberries, to serve
finely chopped rosemary needles,
    to serve

FOR THE ROSEMARY AND
ALMOND CAKES
65g ground almonds
1 tsp finely chopped rosemary
    needles
2 tbsp plain flour
90g caster sugar
2 egg whites
65g butter
oil, for greasing

This is one of those classic ice creams that I often enjoyed out of a cone as a child. It was generally bright, bright green and had some rather sugary 'chocolate' in it. This recipe uses only fresh mint, thus has a different colour and more natural flavour.

MINT CHOCOLATE CHIP ICE CREAM

Put the milk, double cream, honey, condensed milk and mint leaves in a large bowl. Blend using a stick blender until the mint has broken down, then cover the bowl and leave to infuse in the fridge for at least 12 hours.

Strain the mix through a fine sieve into a metal or plastic freezerproof container. Cover and freeze for about 1½ hours, until the base and sides are starting to freeze. Remove from the freezer and vigorously stir with a balloon whisk (or an electric whisk) until smooth. Refreeze, then repeat three or four more times at hourly intervals so that you end up with a smooth, creamy ice cream. On the last stir, mix in the chocolate. If you have an ice-cream machine, follow the manufacturer's instructions and you should have softly frozen ice cream within about 20 minutes.

Serves: 4–6
Preparation time: 5 minutes, plus
    12 hours infusing and freezing

300ml milk
300ml double cream
25g runny honey
200g condensed milk
2 bunches of mint (about 40g), leaves
    only
100g dark chocolate (minimum 70%
    cocoa solids), grated or finely
    chopped

If you have not tried brown bread ice cream before then do give this recipe a try. The crunchy pieces of caramelised brown bread are a great addition to the ice cream and it's a good way to use up any stale bread.

BROWN BREAD ICE CREAM

Put the slices of bread in a food processor and pulse until they form very coarse breadcrumbs.

Put the caster sugar in a small heavy-based saucepan or frying pan. Place over medium heat and leave the sugar to melt and caramelise to a deep golden colour, swirling the pan occasionally to get even caramelisation (do not stir). Add the butter and table salt and whisk to combine well. Add the breadcrumbs and stir using a spatula to coat them well, then transfer to a sheet of baking parchment to cool. When cool, chop into a coarse crumb, either by hand or in a food processor.

Bring the milk and cream to the boil in a medium saucepan, stirring frequently.

Put the egg yolks, soft dark brown sugar, malt extract and honey in a heatproof bowl set over a pan of simmering water (making sure the bottom of the bowl doesn't touch the water) and whisk to combine. Gradually pour the hot milk mixture into the hot egg yolk mixture, whisking continuously, then return the mixture to the pan and cook over very low heat, stirring constantly, until the mixture coats the back of a wooden spoon. Strain through a sieve and allow to cool. Chill in the fridge.

Once chilled, pour the mixture into a metal or plastic freezerproof container. Cover and freeze for about 1½ hours, until the base and sides are starting to freeze. Remove from the freezer and vigorously stir with a balloon whisk (or an electric whisk) until smooth. Refreeze, then repeat twice more at hourly intervals. Add the caramelised breadcrumbs then repeat the freezing and stirring twice more. If you have an ice-cream machine, follow the manufacturer's instructions, adding the caramelised breadcrumbs when the mix is beginning to freeze, and you should have softly frozen ice cream within about 20 minutes.

Serves: 4
Preparation time: 25 minutes, plus
     chilling and freezing

75g stale brown bread slices
50g caster sugar
25g butter, diced
½ tsp table salt
250ml milk
250ml double cream
6 egg yolks
50g soft dark brown sugar
1 tsp malt extract
1 tbsp blossom honey

A well-made pavlova is something rather special. Generally, slightly old egg whites work better than super-fresh whites, so if you have some eggs that are getting near their use-by date, this is a great way to use them up. Always ensure the bowl you use to whip egg whites is very clean and free from any grease otherwise you will struggle to form stiff peaks.

MANGO, PASSION FRUIT AND MINT PAVLOVA

Preheat the oven to 120°C/100°C fan/gas ½ and line a large baking sheet with non-stick baking parchment. Draw a 25cm circle on the paper.

To make the meringue, rub the lemon wedge around the inside of a clean mixing bowl or the bowl of a standmixer. Add the egg whites and whisk on low-medium speed until they form stiff peaks. Increase the mixing speed to high and gradually add the sugar, whisking continuously. Whisk for 10–15 minutes until you have a stiff meringue and all grains of sugar have dissolved.

Dollop spoonfuls of the meringue mixture onto the parchment-lined baking sheet to form a ring shape (there shouldn't be gaps between the dollops).

Bake in the oven for 1 hour or until crisp on the outside, then turn off the oven and leave the door ajar until the pavlova has cooled.

Whisk the mascarpone in a bowl until smooth. Add the rum (if using) and mix well. Lightly whip the double cream until it forms soft peaks, then fold it into the mascarpone mix.

Dollop the cream on the pavlova, top with the diced mango, passion fruit flesh and finely chopped mint and serve.

Serves: 6–8
Preparation time: 20 minutes
Cooking time: 1 hour, plus cooling

100g mascarpone
15ml white rum (optional)
100ml double cream
1 ripe mango, peeled and diced
2 passion fruit
¼ bunch of mint, leaves finely
   chopped

FOR THE MERINGUE
1 lemon wedge
4 egg whites, at room temperature
220g caster sugar

Rose water is not everyone's cup of tea. When it is poor quality, or over-used, it can end up making a dish smell and taste like a perfumery. If it is really not your thing, substitute with limoncello, which works well with the rhubarb. There are two types of rhubarb available throughout the seasons: the vibrant pink variety from Yorkshire, which is grown indoors, and the redder outdoor variety.

RHUBARB AND ROSE TRIFLE

To cook the rhubarb, put the caster sugar and grenadine in a large saucepan. Top up with 500ml water and bring to a simmer, stirring to dissolve the sugar. Place the rhubarb pieces in the hot liquid and simmer for 3 minutes, then remove the pan from the heat and allow the rhubarb to continue to cook in the liquid for 10 minutes, as it cools down. Carefully transfer the rhubarb from the liquid into a bowl, using a slotted spoon and chill. Measure out 400ml of the cooking liquor, place it in a medium saucepan and set aside.

To make the sponge, preheat the oven to 180°C/160°C fan/gas 4. Grease a 20cm square cake tin and line it with baking parchment.

Beat the eggs in a bowl with an electric whisk or in the bowl of a standmixer for 3–5 minutes, until pale and fluffy. Add the sugar and beat for a further 5–7 minutes until smooth and glossy. Gently fold in the flour and ground almonds. Finally, fold in the melted butter.

Transfer the sponge batter to the prepared cake tin and bake for 15–20 minutes, until golden and risen and a skewer inserted into the centre of the sponge comes out clean. Remove from the oven and leave to cool in the tin for 10 minutes, then remove the sponge from the tin and leave it to cool fully on a wire rack. When cold, cut it into 1.5cm cubes.

To make the jelly, soak the 3 gelatine leaves in a bowl of cold water for 5 minutes. Heat the 400ml of rhubarb cooking liquor until it just reaches the boil, then remove the pan from the heat. Squeeze the excess water from the gelatine leaves and stir them into the hot liquid until completely dissolved. Strain the liquid into a clean container, which gives the jelly at least 1cm height, and chill until set.

Serves: 6–8
Preparation time: around 1 hour, plus chilling and cooling
Cooking time: around 25 minutes

200g caster sugar
2 tbsp grenadine
6 rhubarb stalks, trimmed and cut into 2cm lengths
3 gelatine leaves
dried rose petals, to serve (optional)

FOR THE SPONGE
2 eggs
75g caster sugar
90g plain flour, sifted
25g ground almonds
50g butter, melted, plus extra for greasing

FOR THE CUSTARD
2 gelatine leaves
150ml milk
150ml double cream
seeds from 1 vanilla pod
4 egg yolks
50g caster sugar
¼ tsp rose water

To make the custard, soak the gelatine leaves in a bowl of cold water for 5 minutes. Put the milk, cream and vanilla seeds in a medium saucepan and bring just to the boil, stirring frequently.

Put the egg yolks and sugar in a heatproof bowl and whisk until smooth. Slowly pour in the hot milk mixture, whisking continuously. Return the mixture back to the pan and cook over very low heat, stirring constantly, for about 5 minutes or until the custard coats the back of a wooden spoon (take care not to boil the custard as the egg yolks will scramble). Add the rose water and mix well. Squeeze the excess water from the gelatine and stir it into the hot custard until completely dissolved. Strain through a sieve into a clean container, cover the surface of the custard with clingfilm (to avoid a skin forming) and chill in the fridge.

To make the cream, whisk the mascarpone and lemon zest together in a bowl until smooth. Add the double cream and whisk until soft peaks form.

To assemble the trifle, place the rhubarb and sponge dice in your trifle bowl. Cut the rhubarb jelly into 1.5cm cubes and add this. Mix very gently. Whisk the custard then pour it on top. Finish with the cream and sprinkle over the dried rose petals, if using. Chill until ready to serve.

FOR THE CREAM
150g mascarpone
grated zest of 1 lemon
200ml double cream

These pastries are inspired by the millefeuille I had in Paris. I have added the flavours of raspberry and rose to my simplified take on the classic. The slight acidity in the raspberries works well with the creamy custard and rose cream.

RASPBERRY AND ROSE PASTRIES

Preheat the oven to 200°C/180°C fan/gas 6 and line a baking sheet with parchment paper.

If you are using rough puff, roll out the pastry on a lightly floured surface to a 3mm-thick rectangle. Place on the lined baking sheet and place in the fridge for 20 minutes to rest. Cut the pastry into twelve 6 x 9cm rectangles and prick them all over with the prongs of a fork. Place back in the fridge for a further 20 minutes. (If you are using a sheet of puff pastry, omit the first chilling stage and just unroll it, cut it into the rectangles, then chill.)

Cover the chilled pastry rectangles with another sheet of parchment and another baking sheet. Bake for 18–20 minutes until golden. Remove from the oven, take off the top baking sheet and sheet of parchment and leave to cool on a wire rack.

To make the custard, put the milk, cream and vanilla seeds in a medium saucepan and bring just to the boil, stirring frequently. Put the egg yolks, sugar and cornflour in a heatproof bowl and whisk until smooth. Slowly pour in a third of the hot milk, whisking continuously. Reduce the heat to medium-low and add the egg mix to the milk mix. Cook over very low heat, stirring constantly, until it comes to the boil, then simmer for 2 minutes until the mixture coats the back of a wooden spoon. Pass the hot custard through a fine sieve into a container, to remove any lumps. Cover the surface of the custard with clingfilm (to prevent a skin forming) and chill.

To make the rose cream, whisk the cream in a bowl until soft peaks form. Add the rose water and whisk until combined. Place in a piping bag and chill.

Makes: 4
Preparation time: 25 minutes, plus
    cooling and chilling
Cooking time: around 20 minutes

1 batch rough puff pastry (see Eccles
    Cakes page 254) or 1 x 320g sheet of
    ready-rolled all-butter puff pastry
flour, for dusting
1 tbsp crystallised rose petals, finely
    chopped, or dried rose petals
200g raspberries

FOR THE CUSTARD
300ml milk
50ml double cream
seeds from 1 vanilla pod
4 egg yolks
60g caster sugar
30g cornflour

FOR THE ROSE CREAM
200ml double cream
¼ tsp rose water (or to taste)

To make the icing, whisk the icing sugar in a bowl with the butter, lemon juice and 1 tablespoon of boiling water until smooth.

Place four of the pastry rectangles on a piece of baking parchment and ice the top. Sprinkle with the rose petals and leave to set.

Place four more pastry rectangles on a tray. Remove the custard from the fridge and transfer it to a bowl. Whisk until smooth and place in a piping bag.

Pipe all of the custard onto four of the rectangles and top with another pastry rectangle. Divide the raspberries between the four rectangles, around the outside of the pastry, then pipe the rose cream between the raspberries. Top with the iced pastry rectangles and gently press. Chill for 20 minutes then serve.

FOR THE ICING
90g icing sugar
1 tbsp soft butter
juice of ½ lemon

Baked Alaska is one of those time-honoured classics. When I made it back in cookery college I thought it was a very clever invention. I have used coffee and chocolate here, which is a little more indulgent than the traditional version of ice cream, sponge and meringue. *See image on following pages.*

ESPRESSO AND CHOCOLATE BAKED ALASKA

Preheat the oven to 180°C/160°C fan/gas 4 and grease an 18 x 9cm loaf tin.

To make the cake, beat the butter and sugar together in a bowl by hand or in the bowl of a standmixer until light and fluffy, then gradually add the eggs, beating well after each one is added.

Melt the chocolate in a heatproof bowl set over a pan of simmering water (making sure the bottom of the bowl doesn't touch the water).

Mix the melted chocolate into the butter and egg mixture, then add the flour and mix until just combined.

Transfer the cake batter to the prepared loaf tin and bake for around 40 minutes, until the cake is just firm and a skewer inserted into the centre comes out clean.

About 10 minutes before the cake is done, make the espresso glaze. Combine the espresso and Kahlua in a small bowl. Remove the cake from the oven and slowly pour the glaze over the cake, covering the surface and allowing it to soak in. Allow to cool in the tin for 15 minutes, then turn out onto a wire rack and leave to cool completely.

While the cake's cooling, make the ice cream. Heat the milk and cream in a medium saucepan until it just reaches boiling point, stirring frequently. Add the ground coffee and remove from the heat. Cover and leave for 10 minutes then place the pan back on the heat and bring just to the boil.

Whisk the egg yolks and demerara sugar in a heatproof bowl, then slowly pour in the hot milk mixture, whisking continuously. Return the mixture to the pan and cook over very low heat, stirring constantly, until it coats the

Serves: 8
Preparation time: 45 minutes, plus cooling and freezing
Cooking time: around 1 hour 15 minutes

FOR THE CHOCOLATE CAKE BASE
100g soft butter, plus extra for greasing
100g caster sugar
2 eggs
40g dark chocolate (70% cocoa solids), broken into pieces
100g self-raising flour

FOR THE ESPRESSO GLAZE
125ml espresso
50ml Kahlua or or other coffee liqueur

back of a wooden spoon. Whisk in the liqueur, strain through a sieve and leave to cool. Chill in the fridge.

Once chilled, pour the mixture into a metal or plastic freezerproof container. Cover and freeze for about 1½ hours, until the base and sides are starting to freeze. Remove from the freezer and vigorously stir with a balloon whisk (or an electric whisk) until smooth. Refreeze, then repeat twice more at hourly intervals. If you have an ice-cream machine, follow the manufacturer's instructions and you should have softly frozen ice cream within about 20 minutes. Transfer to the same loaf tin you used for the cake, lined with a double layer of clingfilm, and leave to set in the freezer for a minimum of 5 hours.

To make the ganache, bring the cream to the boil in a small saucepan. Place the chocolate in a bowl, pour the cream over it, add the butter then cover with clingfilm and leave to sit for 5 minutes. Whisk until combined. Allow to cool until it holds its shape when whisked.

Trim the top of the cooled cake so that it is flat and even, then turn it upside down. Cover the bottom of the cake (which is now the top) with the ganache. Place in the fridge to set.

Lift the clingfilm out of the loaf tin with the ice cream, then carefully tip the ice cream loaf onto the set ganache on the cake, so that it aligns nicely. Place the entire cake and ice cream into the freezer while you make the meringue.

To make the meringue, place the sugar and 3 tablespoons of water in a small saucepan and set over medium-low heat. Stir until the sugar dissolves, then bring to a fast boil, until it reaches 110°C on a sugar thermometer.

In the meantime, whisk the egg whites in a spotlessly clean bowl with an electric whisk, or in the bowl of a standmixer fitted with the whisk attachment, until they form stiff peaks.

When the syrup temperature has reached 110°C on the sugar thermometer, slowly and carefully pour the syrup over the egg whites in a thin stream while continuing to whisk. Continue whisking for up to 10 minutes, until the meringue has cooled.

Preheat the oven to 180°C/160°C fan/gas 4. Remove the ice cream loaf from the freezer and cover with the meringue, creating swirls and peaks as you do so. Place on a baking tray in the oven for 5 minutes then use a blowtorch to brown the meringue until golden. Serve immediately.

FOR THE ICE CREAM
250ml whole milk
250ml double cream
2 tbsp freshly ground coffee beans
6 egg yolks
50g demerara sugar
50ml Kahlua or other coffee liqueur

FOR THE CHOCOLATE GANACHE
60ml whipping cream
60g dark chocolate (70% cocoa
    solids), broken into pieces
10g soft butter

FOR THE ITALIAN MERINGUE
180g caster sugar
3 egg whites

I liken clafoutis to a sweet version of a Yorkshire pudding, but don't tell the French! It is a great dessert to adapt and make with different fruits, such as cherries, apricots and blackberries, so get creative. Caramelising the plums as I have done here really enriches the flavour. Always use the ripest fruit you can find.

PLUM CLAFOUTIS

Lightly grease four 12–13cm ovenproof blini pans or ramekins with butter.

Preheat the oven to 180°C/160°C fan/gas 4.

Put the demerara sugar in a small heavy-based saucepan or frying pan. Place over medium heat and leave to melt and caramelise to a deep golden colour, swirling the pan occasionally (do not stir) to get even caramelisation – this will take 5–8 minutes. Add the butter, whisk well and simmer for 1–2 minutes until well combined.

Pour a quarter of the caramel into each blini pan or ramekin then quickly, while the caramel is still hot, place 3 plum halves, cut side down, into the caramel.

Put the cream, milk, vanilla seeds and lemon zest in a small saucepan and gently bring to the boil. Remove from the heat.

In a deep bowl, whisk together the eggs and sugar. Whisk in the flour, then gradually add the hot milk and cream, whisking continuously.

Pour the batter over the plums in each pan or ramekin then place in the oven for around 15 minutes, until golden and cooked through. Remove from the oven, dust with icing sugar and serve immediately with your favourite ice cream.

Serves: 4
Preparation time: 15 minutes
Cooking time: 20 minutes

50g butter, plus extra for greasing
4 tbsp demerara sugar
6 ripe plums, halved and stones removed
150ml double cream
150ml milk
seeds from 1 vanilla pod
grated zest of 1 lemon
2 eggs
45g caster sugar
45g plain flour
1 tbsp icing sugar, for dusting
ice cream, to serve

This apple pie is much quicker to make than a deep-dish pie and is also delicious. I like to use Pink Lady apples, as they hold their shape well, but you can substitute them with Braeburns. This recipe also works well with pears and stone fruit.

FREEFORM SPICED APPLE PIE

To make the pastry, rub together the flour, sea salt and cold butter in a bowl with your fingertips until the mixture resembles breadcrumbs (or blitz in a food processor). Stir in the sugar and gradually add the beaten egg to form a soft, pliable dough. Gently form the pastry into a ball, flatten it then wrap it in clingfilm and chill for 30 minutes.

Dust a work surface lightly with flour, unwrap the pastry and roll it out to a 4mm-thick circle. Transfer to a baking sheet lined with baking parchment and chill for 20 minutes.

Peel and halve the apples. Remove the cores and cut the apples into 2mm-thick slices. Place in a large bowl and add the sugar, cinnamon, nutmeg, melted butter and marmalade and toss everything together to coat.

Preheat the oven to 200°C/180°C fan/gas 6.

Remove the pastry from the fridge. Leaving a border of approximately 3cm, arrange the apple slices in the centre in a continuous spiral, leaving any juice behind (keep the juice – you'll use it later). Gently gather the border of the pastry in small sections and fold in towards the centre.

Brush the pastry liberally with the milk then sprinkle with the granulated sugar and walnuts.

Bake for 30–35 minutes until the apples are cooked and the pastry is golden.

While the pie is cooking, pour the leftover apple juice into a small saucepan, add the cloudy apple juice and reduce it until it forms a syrup.

Remove the apple pie from the oven, brush it with the apple syrup and leave to cool on a wire rack. Serve with double cream or ice cream.

Serves: 6–8
Preparation time: 25 minutes, plus 50 minutes chilling
Cooking time: 35 minutes

3–4 Pink Lady apples
100g caster sugar
½ tsp ground cinnamon
½ nutmeg, grated
25g butter, melted
1 tbsp orange marmalade
2 tbsp milk
2 tbsp granulated sugar
2 tbsp walnuts, finely chopped
50ml cloudy apple juice
double cream or ice cream, to serve

FOR THE PASTRY
175g plain flour, plus extra for dusting
pinch of sea salt
115g cold butter, diced
50g caster sugar
1 egg, beaten
grated zest of ½ lemon

These puddings are great for all ages. My kids love them, and I do too, and they are quick and simple to make. The melted chocolate and oozy honeycomb make for a delicious treat. They are usually devoured in seconds, which is always a good sign!

BAKED HONEYCOMB PUDDINGS

Preheat the oven to 200°C/180°C fan/gas 6.

Lightly butter four ramekins and sprinkle them evenly with the tablespoon of sugar.

Put the eggs and 40g caster sugar in a mixing bowl and whisk on high speed until light and fluffy.

Melt the 75g butter with the golden syrup in a pan then stir it into the eggs and sugar, and fold in the flour and baking powder.

Put a large spoonful of the pudding mixture into the bottom of the ramekins. Sprinkle the crushed honeycomb on top. Finish by spooning the remaining pudding mix over the honeycomb. Smooth over the surface with a palette knife.

Sit the ramekins on a baking tray and bake for around 15 minutes, until the puddings puff up and become golden.

Remove from the oven and leave the puddings to rest for 1–2 minutes, then dust with cocoa powder and serve with a spoonful of crème fraîche or ice cream.

Serves: 4
Preparation time: 10 minutes
Cooking time: 15 minutes

75g butter, plus extra for greasing
40g caster sugar, plus 1 tbsp extra
2 eggs
40g golden syrup
100g plain flour
1 tsp baking powder
2 x 40g chocolate-covered
    honeycomb bars, roughly chopped
cocoa powder, to dust
crème fraîche or ice cream, to serve

This was one of my favourite cakes as a kid. I have given it a grown-up makeover here with the addition of quite a lot of rum. It enhances the flavour tenfold but if you would rather not use it, just add a little apricot jam to the reduced pineapple juice to make the glaze.

PINEAPPLE UPSIDE-DOWN CAKES WITH RUM CREAM

Drain the tinned pineapple slices, reserving the juice. Put the pineapple rings in a bowl with 75ml of the rum. Cover and chill for 12 hours to marinate. After 12 hours, drain off the marinade, reserving the rum and adding it to the tinned pineapple juice.

Preheat the oven to 180°C/160°C fan/gas 4. Grease the bases of 4 Yorkshire pudding moulds (10cm diameter at the widest point) and line with baking parchment.

Beat together the butter and sugar in a bowl with an electric whisk or in the bowl of a standmixer until light and creamy. Gradually mix in the egg and whisk until smooth. Add the flour and salt, and gently fold together until combined. Add 1½ tablespoons of the reserved pineapple juice and rum.

Divide 1½ tablespoons of the golden syrup between the bottoms of the moulds and place the marinated pineapple slices on top. Gently spread the cake batter on top of the pineapple slices.

Bake in the oven for about 15 minutes, until the cakes are just firm in the centre and a skewer inserted into the middle of each cake comes out clean. Remove from the oven, allow to cool slightly for about 10 minutes, then carefully remove them from the moulds (a palette knife helps to release them easily). Mix the remaining 1 tablespoon of golden syrup into the reserved pineapple juice and rum glaze and brush the top of the pineapple slices.

To make the rum cream, whisk the cream in a bowl until soft peaks form, then add the remaining 15ml of rum and whisk until the cream forms stiff peaks.

Serve the cakes warm with the rum cream.

Makes: 4 individual pineapple cakes
Preparation time: 20 minutes, plus
    12 hours marinating
Cooking time: 35 minutes

1 x 220g tin pineapple rings, in juice
    (4 slices)
90ml dark rum
50g soft butter, plus extra for greasing
50g caster sugar
1 medium egg, lightly beaten
50g self-raising flour
pinch of salt
2½ tbsp golden syrup
100ml double cream

CARAMELISING

Caramelisation is the process of heating sugar, sugar-based products or honey until they become a deep golden brown. This completely alters the structure of the sugar, as well as its flavour, giving it a slightly savoury, richer taste and diluting some of its sweetness. We use it in our rather infamous salted caramel soft serve at Tredwells, as well as a sherry vinegar caramel for a monkfish dish at The Gilbert Scott.

Sugar begins to caramelise and darken at 165°C, at first turning a light golden colour. A golden caramel will start to form at approximately 171°C, with a dark caramel being reached at 180°C. You can use a sugar thermometer; however, it is something you can judge by eye the more you do it.

The important thing to always remember when caramelising sugar is not to stir the sugar at all, as this could cause it to crystallise which will make it impossible to then caramelise. Instead of stirring, gently shake or swirl the pan to redistribute the sugar when it begins to melt. You do have to be patient throughout this process but, as soon as it begins to colour, you need to pay a lot of attention, otherwise – if you leave the pan when it's close to reaching the desired level of caramelisation – it will burn. However, if you're hesitant and do not let the sugar get dark enough, the caramel will be sickly and potentially cause the sauce to be too runny. It can be a fine line!

When making a caramel there needs to be a point where you either stop it cooking by pouring the caramel onto a flat surface, or into a large dish to cool, or you add another ingredient, such as butter or cream, or an alcohol or other liquid. Once you have added the fat or liquid, you can then begin to whisk the caramel. It is crucial that the cream or milk are hot when they are added, as if cold the caramel will seize when the cold liquid hits the hot sugar. Heavy-based pans are ideal, as the heat is distributed a lot more evenly.

KEY TEMPERATURES	Occurrence
70°C	Honey begins to caramelise
110°C	Honey forms a dark caramel
160°C	Sugar begins to melt
165–170°C	Sugar begins to caramelise and form a light caramel
171–179°C	A golden-coloured caramel is forming
180°C	A dark caramel begins to form. If the sugar heats to 186°C or above it will be bitter and burnt

Bananas are one of my favourite ingredients to make sweet treats with. You will always get the best flavour out of them if they are overripe and as black as possible. Adding them to caramel enhances their flavour, too. If you have them in your fruit bowl but do not have time to bake them then just pop them in the freezer until you do. This recipe is dairy and gluten free.

BANANA AND COCONUT CAKE WITH CARAMELISED BANANA COCONUT ICE CREAM

Serves: 8
Preparation time: 30 minutes, plus
   chilling and freezing
Cooking time: 1 hour

3 overripe bananas (about 360g total
   weight), peeled and mashed

FOR THE CARAMELISED BANANA
COCONUT ICE CREAM
80g caster sugar
2 tbsp dark rum
150ml almond milk
350ml coconut milk
6 egg yolks

FOR THE BANANA COCONUT CAKE
6 tbsp coconut oil, plus extra for
   greasing
100g dairy-free coconut yoghurt
5 eggs
70g coconut flour
70g ground almonds
100g cornflour
130g soft light brown sugar
1 tsp baking powder
1 tsp bicarbonate of soda

To make the ice cream, put the caster sugar in a medium heavy-based saucepan or frying pan. Place over medium heat and let the sugar melt and caramelise to a deep golden colour, swirling the pan occasionally so that the sugar caramelises evenly (watch it carefully). Add half of the mashed banana and gently stir. Turn down the heat and cook for a further 15–20 minutes until the banana has broken down and the caramel has formed a purée. Gradually add the rum, almond milk and coconut milk and bring to the boil, stirring frequently.

Whisk the egg yolks in a mixing bowl until well combined. Slowly pour in the hot milk mixture, whisking continuously. Return the mixture back into the pan and cook over very low heat, stirring all the time, until the mixture coats the back of a wooden spoon.

Strain the custard through a sieve into a heatproof bowl and leave to cool. Cover the surface of the custard with clingfilm and chill in the fridge.

Pour the mixture into a metal or plastic freezerproof container. Cover and freeze for about 1½ hours, until the base and sides of the custard are starting to freeze. Remove from the freezer and whisk vigorously with a balloon whisk (or an electric whisk) until smooth. Refreeze, then repeat three or four more times at hourly intervals so that you end up with a smooth, creamy ice cream. If you have an ice-cream machine, follow the manufacturer's instructions and you should have softly frozen ice cream within about 20 minutes.

Preheat the oven to 200°C/180°C fan/gas 6. Grease a 23cm cake tin and line it with baking parchment.

To make the banana cake, put the coconut oil and yoghurt, eggs and the remaining mashed banana in a food processor and blend until smooth. Add the coconut flour, almonds, cornflour, brown sugar, baking powder and bicarbonate of soda, then blend until combined.

Pour the mixture into the prepared tin and smooth over the top.

Bake for about 30 minutes, until golden and just firm to the touch and a skewer inserted into the centre of the sponge comes out clean.

Remove the cake from the oven and allow to cool for 5 minutes before carefully removing from the tin and serving, while warm, with the ice cream.

This may sound unusual, but the high moisture content in courgettes make them a great addition to any cake. The anise caramel also gives it a lovely liquorice-like flavour which works really well with the spices. The cake is a wonderful pale green colour, too.

WARM SPICED COURGETTE CAKE WITH ANISE CARAMEL

Preheat the oven to 180°C/160°C fan/gas 4 and grease a 20cm loose-bottomed or springform cake tin with butter.

Put the grated courgettes in a colander, sprinkle with the table salt and toss to distribute. Set over a bowl or sink and leave for 30 minutes to drain.

Put the courgettes in a clean tea towel and squeeze out as much of the liquid as possible.

Put 175g of the caster sugar and 175g of the butter in a bowl with the lemon zest. Beat until pale and creamy, then mix in the grated courgette and lemon juice and beat in the eggs, one at a time, adding a spoonful of flour with each egg to prevent curdling. Mix in the remaining flour and spices (except the star anise). Transfer to the prepared tin and level with a palette knife.

Bake for 40–50 minutes, or until golden and a skewer inserted into the centre comes out clean. Remove from the oven and leave to cool for 20 minutes, then remove from the tin, turn it over and place it upside down on a wire rack.

Put the remaining 50g of caster sugar in a small heavy-based saucepan or frying pan with the star anise. Place over medium heat and let the sugar melt to a deep golden colour, swirling the pan occasionally so that the sugar caramelises evenly (watch it carefully and don't stir). Remove from the heat, add the remaining 25g butter and whisk to combine. Add 4 tablespoons of boiling water (be careful, it will bubble up) and swirl the pan again. Return to low-medium heat and simmer for 3–5 minutes, until any solidified sugar has dissolved and it has thickened slightly. Strain through a fine sieve into a clean saucepan.

To serve, place the just-warm cake on a serving plate right side up then drizzle it with the warm caramel, slice and serve with crème fraîche.

Serves: 10–12
Preparation time: 20 minutes, plus 20 minutes salting
Cooking time: 50 minutes, plus cooling

200g soft unsalted butter, plus extra for greasing
3 medium courgettes, coarsely grated
1 tsp table salt
225g caster sugar
grated zest and juice of 1 lemon
2 eggs
220g self-raising flour
½ tsp ground ginger
½ tsp ground cinnamon
½ tsp Chinese five-spice powder
2 star anise, ground to a powder in a spice grinder or pestle and mortar
crème fraîche, to serve

Baking brioche at home fills the house with the most amazing smell. It is difficult to resist temptation and let the loaf cool before slicing into it, but do try as it can tend to clump together if you slice it when hot. The dates and orange blossom water add a slight Middle Eastern twist. The brioche dough requires a standmixer, as it's very sticky.

DATE AND ORANGE BLOSSOM BRIOCHE

Put the chopped dates in a small saucepan. Cover with water and place over high heat. Bring to the boil for 2 minutes then remove and set aside to soak for 20 minutes. Drain thoroughly through a sieve then put them in a bowl and add the orange blossom water.

To make the brioche dough, place the flour, yeast, sugar and table salt in the bowl of a standmixer fitted with the dough hook and combine, then add the milk, orange zest and 3 whole eggs and mix until you have a soft, smooth dough that leaves the sides of the bowl. Knead with the dough hook for 7–10 minutes.

Gradually add the butter to the dough, a little at a time, until the dough has absorbed it all.

Cover the bowl with lightly oiled clingfilm and leave in a warm place for about 1½ hours, or until the dough has doubled in size.

Add the dates to the dough and work them in until just combined. Don't be alarmed if the dough is very wet and sticky – this is normal.

Grease a 1kg loaf tin and line it with baking parchment. Tip the bread dough into the tin and level the top, then cover with lightly oiled clingfilm and leave in a warm place to prove for 30–45 minutes.

Preheat the oven to 200°C/180°C fan/gas 6.

Brush the top of the loaf with the egg yolk then bake for 20–25 minutes, cover with foil and bake for a further 20 minutes, until golden and cooked through. Remove from the oven, tip out of the tin and leave to cool on a wire rack.

Makes: 1 loaf
Preparation time: 20 minutes, plus 1½ hours rising and 45 minutes proving
Cooking time: 45 minutes

100g dried soft dates, stones removed, roughly chopped
dash of orange blossom water (or to taste)
350g strong white bread flour
7g sachet fast-action dried yeast or easy-bake yeast
1 tbsp caster sugar
1 tsp table salt
70ml milk
grated zest of 1 orange
3 eggs, plus 1 egg yolk
80g soft butter, plus extra for greasing

These baps are great to enjoy with your choice of sandwich fillings, but they are also very tasty just on their own, or served with soup for a satisfying winter supper. Caramelising the onions brings out their sweetness, just take care to cook them slowly to get as much colour as possible, without burning them.

CARAMELISED ONION, ROSEMARY AND PARMESAN BAPS

To make the dough, put 500g of the flour in a bowl and mix in the yeast, sugar, rosemary and salt. Make a well in the centre and pour in the milk, olive oil and 250ml of warm water. Mix together until you have a smooth, wet dough. Turn out onto a lightly floured surface and knead for 7–10 minutes until soft and smooth, adding more flour if necessary. Alternatively, make the dough in a standmixer fitted with a dough hook.

Transfer the dough to a clean, lightly oiled bowl, cover the bowl with lightly oiled clingfilm and leave to rest in a warm place for 1–1½ hours, or until the dough has doubled in size.

While the dough is rising, melt 25g of the butter in a medium frying pan over medium-high heat. When hot, add the onions, season with salt, and cook for 15–20 minutes until the onions are brown and caramelised (but not burnt), adding the remaining butter if needed. Add the balsamic vinegar and cook for a further 3 minutes. Season well with black pepper and remove from the heat.

Turn out the risen dough, knock it back and knead it for a couple of minutes, then add half of the grated Parmesan and knead for another couple of minutes to work the cheese into the dough. Divide the dough into eight balls. Roll out each ball to a thickness of 1cm and transfer to two floured baking trays. Cover the trays loosely with clingfilm and leave to rest in a warm place for 30 minutes.

Preheat the oven to 200°C/180°C fan/gas 6. Remove the clingfilm from the baps and brush each one generously with milk. Top with the caramelised onions and the remaining Parmesan. Bake for 25–30 minutes until lightly golden and cooked through (they should sound hollow when tapped on the base).

Makes: 8 baps
Preparation time: 25 minutes, plus
    1½–2 hours rising
Cooking time: around 50 minutes

40g butter
2 onions, finely sliced
1 tbsp balsamic vinegar
100g finely grated Parmesan
freshly ground black pepper

FOR THE DOUGH
500–600g strong white bread flour
7g sachet fast-action dried yeast or
    easy-bake yeast
1 tbsp caster sugar
1 tbsp rosemary needles, finely
    chopped
2 tsp table salt, plus extra for
    seasoning
100ml milk, plus extra for glazing
75ml olive oil, plus extra for greasing

Putting baked potatoes in a bread dough may seem a little odd, but do give this recipe a try as it is one of my favourites. The earthy flavour of the potato skins works really well, and the potato flesh adds a lovely texture to the bread, too.

SAFFRON AND POTATO BREAD

Preheat the oven to 200°C/180°C fan/gas 6.

Scrub the potato and prick it all over. Place it in a roasting tray and bake in the oven for 1 hour 20 minutes, or until cooked all the way through. Remove from the oven and break it open, allowing the steam to escape and the potato to cool.

Put the saffron strands in a heatproof bowl and add 250ml of hot (but not boiling) water and stir well. Set aside to infuse for 10 minutes.

To make the dough, put the flour in a bowl and mix in the yeast, sugar and salt. Pour in the olive oil and the saffron water, mix together and knead until you have a smooth, wet dough. Turn out onto a lightly floured surface and knead for 7–10 minutes until soft and smooth, adding more flour if necessary. Alternatively, make the dough in a standmixer fitted with a dough hook.

Transfer the dough to a clean, lightly oiled bowl, cover the bowl with lightly oiled clingfilm and leave to rest in a warm place for 1–1½ hours, or until the dough has doubled in size.

Roughly chop the potato, leaving the skin on, into 1–2cm chunks, then mix the chunks into the dough. Tip the bread dough out onto a floured work surface and roll it into a loaf shape. Place on an oiled baking tray, cover with clingfilm and put in a warm place to prove for 30 minutes.

Bake the bread for around 1 hour 15 minutes, covering loosely with foil after 40 minutes to prevent it burning on top, until golden brown and cooked through (it should sound hollow when tapped on the base).

Makes: 1 large loaf
Preparation time: 20 minutes plus 1½ hours rising and 30 minutes proving
Cooking time: 2 hours 25 minutes

1 large baking potato (around 350g)
pinch of saffron strands
500g strong white bread flour, plus extra for dusting
7g sachet fast-action dried yeast or easy-bake yeast
1 tbsp caster sugar
2 tsp table salt, plus extra for seasoning
50ml olive oil, plus extra for greasing

Fermentation has become quite a buzzword lately, yet it is a technique that has been used for centuries and many of the foods we already eat, such as cheese, wine and pickles, are fermented. The barley in this recipe takes on a lovely, slightly sour flavour.

FERMENTED BARLEY AND ALE BREAD

Put the barley in a bowl and cover with water. Wrap the bowl loosely in clingfilm and leave for 2–3 days at room temperature until the water starts to foam. The longer you leave it, the stronger the ferment will taste.

Rinse the fermented barley under cold running water and put it in a small saucepan. Cover with cold water and cook according to the packet instructions (around 40 minutes). Strain and allow to steam-dry.

Combine the strong white flour, rye flour, table salt, yeast and drained barley in a bowl. Mix the ale, olive oil and malt extract and mix it into the flour, then knead for about 10 minutes to form a soft, smooth dough that leaves the sides of the bowl. (This can be done by hand or using a standmixer fitted with a dough hook.) Add more strong white flour if needed.

Cover the bowl with lightly oiled clingfilm and leave somewhere warm for about 1 hour, or until the dough has doubled in size.

Tip the dough out onto a floured work surface and shape it into a large circle. Place on an oiled baking tray. Cover with clingfilm and place somewhere warm to prove for 30 minutes.

Preheat the oven to 200°C/180°C fan/gas 6.

Bake the bread for 50 minutes–1 hour, until lightly golden and it sounds hollow when tapped on the base, covering the bread with foil for the last 20 minutes of cooking time if it's getting too brown. Remove from the oven and leave to cool completely on a wire rack before slicing.

Makes: 1 loaf
Preparation time: 15 minutes, plus 2–3 days fermenting, minimum 1 hour rising and 30 minutes proving
Cooking time: 1 hour 45 minutes

100g pearl barley
400g strong white flour, plus extra for dusting
100g rye flour
2 tsp table salt
7g sachet fast-action dried yeast or easy-bake yeast
300ml ale
50ml olive oil, plus extra for greasing
1 tbsp malt extract

Gluten-free bread has traditionally been rather cardboard-like in texture. Here, however, a mixture of cornflour and gluten-free flour gives the bread a more moisture-rich consistency. The pumpkin seeds also add a lovely nuttiness to the loaf.

GLUTEN-FREE PUMPKIN-SEED BREAD

Grease an 18 x 9cm loaf tin and line it with baking parchment.

Mix the yeast, maple syrup, olive oil and 350ml of warm water in a bowl until the yeast has dissolved.

In a separate, larger bowl, mix together the cornflour, gluten-free flour, xanthan gum, salt and pumpkin seeds. Pour in the yeast mixture, then mix well to make a smooth, thin batter.

Leave the batter for 5–10 minutes for the liquid to form into a sticky dough as the cornflour and xanthan gum absorb the liquid and become gel-like in consistency.

Cover the bowl with a piece of oiled clingfilm and leave the dough to prove in a warm place for 30 minutes, until it has risen by about a third.

Transfer the risen dough to the prepared tin and brush it with olive oil. Cover with a piece of oiled clingfilm and leave in a warm place for a further 30 minutes.

Preheat the oven to 200°C/180°C fan/gas 6.

Bake for 40–50 minutes, until the loaf is golden and sounds hollow when tapped on the base. Remove from the oven and leave to cool in the tin for 20 minutes, then place on a wire rack and leave to cool completely.

Makes: 1 loaf
Preparation time: 5 minutes, plus
    1 hour rising and proving
Cooking time: 50 minutes

50ml olive oil, plus extra for brushing
7g sachet fast-action dried yeast or
    easy-bake yeast
1 tbsp maple syrup
170g cornflour
120g gluten-free plain white flour
7g xanthan gum
1 tsp table salt
100g pumpkin seeds, toasted and
    finely chopped

Love it or hate it, Marmite is a great flavour enhancer when it's used in cooking. This bread reminds me of my childhood and having warm Marmite on toast for an afternoon snack after school.

MARMITE, ONION AND CHEDDAR BREAD

Mix together the flour, yeast, sugar, salt, olive oil and 300ml of warm water in a bowl to form a soft dough that leaves the sides of the bowl. Knead for 7–10 minutes, until smooth. This can be done by hand or using a standmixer fitted with a dough hook.

Cover the bowl with lightly oiled clingfilm and leave in a warm place for about 1 hour, or until the dough has doubled in size.

While the dough is proving, melt the butter in a medium frying pan over medium-high heat. When hot, add the onions, season with salt and cook for 15–20 minutes until the onions are caramelised.

Tip the dough out onto a floured work surface and roll it into a large rectangle, approximately 1cm thick. Leaving a 4cm border on one edge, spread the Marmite onto the dough. Top with the caramelised onions and spread them out evenly, then sprinkle over the grated cheese. Carefully roll the bread in on itself, leaving the border exposed. Brush the border with warm water, then fold over the top of the dough. Roll the bread until the seal is underneath. Fold under each of the ends of the bread and place it on an oiled baking tray. Cover with clingfilm and leave in a warm place to prove for 30 minutes.

Preheat the oven to 200°C/180°C fan/gas 6.

Brush the bread with milk and sprinkle a little more cheese over the top. Season well with black pepper.

Bake the bread for 20–25 minutes, then cover it loosely with foil and bake a further 20–25 minutes, until cooked through. Remove from the oven and leave to cool on a wire rack before slicing.

Makes: 1 large loaf
Preparation time: 15 minutes, plus 1 hour rising and 30 minutes proving
Cooking time: 1 hour 10 minutes

500g strong white bread flour
7g sachet fast-action dried yeast or easy-bake yeast
1 tbsp caster sugar
2 tsp table salt, plus extra for seasoning
50ml olive oil, plus extra for greasing
25g butter
2 onions, finely sliced
2 tbsp Marmite, warmed slightly
100g Cheddar cheese, grated, plus extra for sprinkling
2 tbsp milk
freshly ground black pepper

Warm cheese straws served with soup for a winter supper is a great treat. I have added blue cheese to this recipe which gives them a more earthy flavour. Try them with the Celeriac and Apple Soup with Smoked Crème Fraîche on page 22.

BLUE CHEESE STRAWS

Combine the flour, table salt, thyme leaves and a good twist of black pepper together in a bowl. Add the cold grated butter and rub it into the flour with your fingertips until the mixture resembles breadcrumbs. Mix in 60g of the blue cheese then bind with the milk to make a stiff dough. If it doesn't come together, add a little more milk. Form the dough into a rectangle, wrap it in clingfilm and chill for 30 minutes.

Preheat the oven to 210°C/190°C fan/gas 7 and dust two baking trays with flour.

Dust a work surface with flour, unwrap the dough and roll it out to a rectangle shape, about 5mm thick. Cut into 18–20 long strips about 1cm wide.

Lay the strips on the floured baking trays, brush with milk then twist each strip lightly. Crumble the remaining cheese over the straws and finish with a good twist of black pepper.

Bake for 15–20 minutes until golden, swapping the trays around halfway through the baking time to ensure the straws cook evenly. Remove from the oven and serve warm or cool.

Makes: 18–20 straws
Preparation time: 15 minutes, plus 30 minutes chilling
Cooking time: around 20 minutes

250g plain white flour, plus extra for dusting
½ tsp table salt
1 tsp thyme leaves
125g cold butter, grated
80g Stilton (or other similar blue cheese), crumbled
2 tbsp milk, plus extra for glazing
freshly ground black pepper

These savoury scones are a great hit in my household, but be warned: they're so delicious that they won't last long! You can substitute the courgette with other vegetables, such as carrot, parsnip and aubergine, and try different cheeses to create new flavours.

COURGETTE, TARRAGON AND CHEESE SCONES

Preheat the oven to 200°C/180°C fan/gas 6 and lightly dust a baking tray with flour.

Put the grated courgettes in a colander, sprinkle with the table salt and toss to distribute the salt. Set the colander over a bowl or the sink and leave for 30 minutes to drain.

Put the grated courgettes in a clean tea towel and squeeze out as much of the liquid as possible.

Put the flour and tarragon in a bowl and rub in the butter with your fingertips until the mixture resembles breadcrumbs. Mix in 75g of the grated cheese and the courgettes and a generous amount of black pepper. Gradually add the milk, mixing it for just long enough to bring everything together into a firm dough (be careful not to overmix).

Dust the work surface with flour, then tip the dough out onto the surface and roll it out to a thickness of 5cm. Cover loosely with clingfilm and leave to rest for 10 minutes before cutting into six squares.

Transfer the scones to the lightly floured baking tray and sprinkle them with the remaining grated cheese and more black pepper. Bake for 25–30 minutes, until the scones are golden and cooked through. Remove from the oven and transfer to a wire rack to cool.

Makes: 6 scones

Preparation time: 15 minutes, plus 30 minutes salting

Cooking time: 30 minutes

250g self-raising flour, plus extra for dusting

300g courgettes, coarsely grated

2½ tsp table salt

2 tbsp finely chopped tarragon

75g cold butter, grated

100g grated Cheddar cheese

75ml milk

freshly ground black pepper

Instead of the usual raspberry jam, I have used blackcurrant jam. It is more aromatic than raspberry jam and has a balanced acidity which I think works very well with the sweet crispness of the biscuits and the buttery icing. These are best eaten on the day they are made.

VIENNESE WHIRLS

Preheat the oven to 180°C/160°C fan/gas 4.

To make the biscuits, beat the butter and icing sugar together in a bowl until soft and fluffy. Combine the flour, cornflour and salt in a separate bowl, then add to the creamed butter and mix until it comes together into a dough.

Spoon the biscuit dough into a piping bag fitted with a star nozzle and pipe 18 x 5cm circles onto baking trays.

Bake for 12 minutes, until just golden and crisp. Remove and transfer to a wire rack to cool.

To make the icing, beat the butter, icing sugar and vanilla seeds together in a bowl until light and fluffy. Add the crème de cassis, if using, and beat until combined.

Spread a small amount of jam onto the bottom of half of the biscuits. Spread a small amount of icing on the remaining biscuits then sandwich them together to make nine biscuits. Dust with the icing sugar before serving.

Makes: 9 biscuits
Preparation time: 20 minutes
Cooking time: 12 minutes, plus
    cooling

FOR THE BISCUITS
250g soft butter
60g icing sugar, sifted
200g plain flour
80g cornflour
pinch of table salt

FOR THE ICING
100g soft butter
125g icing sugar, sifted, plus extra for
    dusting
seeds from 1 vanilla pod
1 tbsp crème de cassis (optional)

4 tbsp blackcurrant jam

This is one of my all-time favourite recipes. It is very satisfying to make your own rough puff pastry at home, and even more so when you get to eat it with such a delicious filling. Try not to over-handle the dough – if it gets too warm while you're making it, the butter in it will start melting and the pastry will become too soft to handle. I add lots of nutmeg to my recipe as it's my favourite spice.

ECCLES CAKES

Start by making the pastry. Remove the butter from the fridge 10 minutes before you start. Sift the flour and salt into a bowl and, using your fingertips, partially rub in the butter, leaving small lumps. Add 100–125ml of iced water and mix together until a stiff dough forms. Tip the dough out onto a floured work surface and shape it into a rectangle 4cm deep. Transfer the dough to a floured tray, cover with clingfilm and chill for 30 minutes.

Transfer the chilled block of pastry onto a floured work surface and roll it out to a rectangle measuring 20 x 15cm. Fold in the quarter of the pastry furthest away from you to meet the middle, and repeat with the quarter of pastry nearest you, so you have what looks like an open book. Fold the book in half lengthways, then transfer it back to the floured tray, cover with clingfilm and chill for 30 minutes.

Repeat the above step twice more.

Finally, place the chilled pastry rectangle on a floured work surface and roll it out to 5mm thickness. Cut it in half then place each half between two sheets of baking parchment, cover with clingfilm and chill for 30 minutes.

While the pastry is chilling, make the filling. Put the butter, sugar, orange zest, cinnamon and nutmeg in a small saucepan over medium heat. Cook until the butter has melted and the sugar has dissolved, stirring frequently. Put the golden raisins, currants and mixed peel in a large bowl and mix together with the spiced butter. Cover and chill.

Makes: 12
Preparation time: 40 minutes, plus
    2 hours 50 minutes folding, rolling
    and chilling
Cooking time: 15–20 minutes

milk, for glazing
granulated sugar, for sprinkling

FOR THE ROUGH PUFF PASTRY
250g butter, diced and chilled
250g plain white flour, plus extra for
    dusting
½ tsp table salt

When the filling mix is cool, divide it into twelve balls. Roll out each ball and flatten them to create discs 4.5–5cm in diameter. Place on a sheet of baking parchment and chill.

Transfer the chilled pastry back to the floured work surface and cut out 12 discs, approximately 9cm in diameter. Place the discs on the floured tray and chill.

To assemble, take two pastry discs out of the fridge at a time. Place a disc of the fruit filling in the centre of each then begin to fold the edges of the pastry disc over the filling, using your index finger to fold over a little pastry, repeating the folding to enclose the filling. Press to seal, then turn the filled disc over and flatten it a little with your hand. Place back in the fridge. Leave them all in the fridge for another 20 minutes before baking.

Preheat the oven to 230°C/210°C fan/gas 8 and line a baking tray with baking parchment.

Place the cakes on the lined tray and brush them liberally with milk. Sprinkle each one with granulated sugar then, using a sharp knife, make three even-sized and evenly spaced incisions in the centre of each cake.

Bake for 15–20 minutes until golden, then remove and transfer to a wire rack.

FOR THE FILLING
55g butter
55g demerara sugar
grated zest of 1 orange
¾ tsp ground cinnamon
½ nutmeg, freshly grated
55g golden raisins
55g currants
35g mixed peel, finely chopped

Bourbon creams don't usually contain bourbon, but I have included it in the icing in this recipe as it really adds to the richness. If you don't have a rectangular biscuit cutter, just cut the biscuit dough into rectangles with a knife.

BOURBON AND PECAN CREAMS

To make the biscuits, beat the diced butter, caster sugar and dark brown sugar together in a bowl by hand or in the bowl of a standmixer until soft and fluffy. Add the maple syrup and mix to combine, then sift the flour and cocoa powder together into the mixture and mix again. Heat the milk until tepid and whisk in the bicarbonate of soda. Add this to the biscuit mixture and combine.

Shape the dough into a rectangle, wrap in clingfilm and chill for 30 minutes.

Preheat the oven to 180°C/160°C fan/gas 4 and line a baking tray with baking parchment.

Unwrap the dough, cut it in half and re-wrap one half, putting it back in the fridge. On a floured surface, roll out the other half of dough into a 3mm-thick rectangle, trimming the edges if needed. Using a straight or fluted rectangular cutter, or a sharp knife, cut 2.5 x 5.5cm rectangles out of the pastry and transfer them to the lined baking tray. Repeat with the other half of the dough. You should be able to get 24–28 rectangles out of each half of dough. Chill the cut biscuits for 15–20 minutes.

Bake the chilled biscuits for 7–10 minutes until they have firmed up and puffed up. Their centres will be slightly soft, but will firm up once cool. Remove from the oven and transfer to a wire rack.

While the biscuits are cooling, make the filling. Place the pecan nuts on a baking tray and roast for 6–10 minutes until golden. Remove from the oven and allow to cool then very finely chop (or blitz in a food processor).

Beat the butter and sugars together in a bowl by hand or in the bowl of a standmixer until soft and fluffy. Add the bourbon and maple syrup and mix well. Mix in the chopped or ground pecan nuts then transfer the icing to a piping bag.

Ice the underside of half the biscuits then sandwich the other halves on top. Dust with cocoa powder to serve.

Makes: 24–28 biscuits
Preparation time: 40 minutes, plus
    50 minutes chilling
Cooking time: 20 minutes, plus
    cooling

FOR THE BISCUITS
100g soft butter, diced
50g caster sugar
50g soft dark brown sugar
2 tbsp maple syrup
200g plain flour, plus extra for
    dusting
40g cocoa powder, plus extra for
    dusting
2 tbsp milk
½ tsp bicarbonate of soda

FOR THE FILLING
50g pecan nuts
75g soft butter
50g icing sugar
50g soft dark brown sugar
1 tbsp bourbon
2 tbsp maple syrup

These cookies are quick and easy to make and are great to try with kids. The thyme adds an interesting dimension to the mix. They will keep well in an airtight container for up to five days.

OAT, MACADAMIA AND APRICOT COOKIES

Preheat the oven to 180°C/160°C fan/gas 4 and grease a baking sheet.

Combine the flour, sugar, oats, macadamia nuts, apricots, cinnamon and thyme in a bowl.

Melt the butter in a pan with the golden syrup. Add the bicarbonate of soda to 2 tablespoons of just-boiled water then mix it into the butter and golden syrup.

Remove from the heat and mix the wet ingredients into the dry ingredients.

Divide the mixture into eight balls and flatten them on the greased baking sheet. Bake for 10–15 minutes until golden. Remove from the oven and transfer to a wire rack to cool.

Makes: 8 large cookies
Preparation time: 10 minutes
Cooking time: 15 minutes

120g plain flour
60g caster sugar
65g jumbo rolled oats
50g macadamia nuts, roughly chopped
50g dried apricots, roughly chopped
½ tsp ground cinnamon
½ tsp thyme leaves
70g butter, plus extra for greasing
2 tbsp golden syrup
½ tsp bicarbonate of soda

This is a slightly different version of a traditional scone. The buttermilk makes them a little more moist and the golden syrup adds a lovely caramel flavour – don't worry, you can still eat them with a big dollop of jam and clotted cream. When making scones, take care not to overmix the dough, to ensure they are light and fluffy.

BUTTERMILK AND GOLDEN SYRUP SCONES

Preheat the oven to 200°C/180°C fan/gas 6 and lightly dust a baking tray with flour.

Combine the flour and salt in a bowl and rub in the butter with your fingertips until the mixture resembles breadcrumbs.

Whisk 3 tablespoons of the golden syrup into the buttermilk then gradually add to the flour mix, mixing it for just long enough to bring everything together into a firm dough (be careful not to overmix).

Dust the work surface with flour, then tip the dough out onto the surface and roll it out to a thickness of 4–5cm. Cover loosely with clingfilm, leave to rest for 10 minutes then cut it into six squares using a sharp knife.

Transfer the scones to the floured baking tray and bake for 15 minutes. Remove the tray from the oven and drizzle the remaining 2 tablespoons of golden syrup over the scones. Return the tray to the oven for a further 5–10 minutes, until the scones are golden and cooked through. Remove from the oven and transfer the scones to a wire rack to cool.

Makes: 6 scones
Preparation time: 10 minutes plus resting time
Cooking time: 25 minutes

250g self-raising flour, plus extra for dusting
½ tsp table salt
75g cold butter, grated
5 tbsp golden syrup
120ml buttermilk

This is a rather decadent treat, and it's well worth the effort. I prefer my meringues slightly soft in the centre, but if you prefer them crisp, bake them for a little longer. You can make the meringues a day or two ahead, storing them in an airtight container once cool, until ready to serve. If you have any leftover almond paste, try it on warm toast as an indulgence.

TOASTED ALMOND MERINGUES

Preheat the oven to 140°C/120°C fan/gas 1 and line a baking tray with baking parchment.

To make the meringue, whisk the egg whites in a spotlessly clean bowl with an electric whisk (or in a standmixer) on medium speed until they form stiff peaks. Increase the speed to high and gradually add the caster sugar, whisking continuously for 3–5 minutes until you have a stiff meringue. Add the icing sugar and beat until just combined (the icing sugar makes the meringue softer).

Spoon the meringue mixture into a piping bag fitted with a 1cm nozzle and pipe 3cm rounds onto the parchment-lined baking tray – you should get about 24 circles. Using a Microplane grater, grate the whole almonds over the top of the meringues. Bake in the oven for 45 minutes, then open the door slightly and turn the oven off. Leave to cool for a further 30 minutes then remove from the oven to cool completely.

To make the almond paste, preheat the oven to 200°C/180°C fan/gas 6. Spread the flaked almonds out in a baking tray and roast for 8–10 minutes until a deep golden colour. Remove from the oven, transfer to a blender or food processor, add the honey, butter, milk and salt and blend until a smooth paste forms.

Whisk the double cream in a bowl until it forms soft peaks. Add the Amaretto or almond liqueur and whisk to form stiff peaks.

Spread a little of the almond paste onto the bottom of each meringue. Add a teaspoon of whipped cream to half of the meringue bases then sandwich them together with another meringue.

Makes: 12 meringues
Preparation time: 20 minutes
Cooking time: 45 minutes, plus cooling

FOR THE MERINGUE
3 egg whites
75g caster sugar
75g icing sugar, sifted
25g whole almonds, skin on

FOR THE ALMOND PASTE
100g flaked almonds
2 tbsp runny honey
20g butter
2–3 tbsp milk
small pinch of table salt

FOR THE AMARETTO CREAM
100ml double cream
1 tbsp Amaretto or almond liqueur

Popcorn, caramel and chocolate. This is a great treat for all ages and is very simple to make. You can pop the popcorn in advance and store in an airtight container. Try adding other ingredients, too – I am partial to the odd marshmallow and raisins as additions.

SALTED CARAMEL AND MILK CHOCOLATE POPCORN BARS

Grease a 20cm square baking tin and line it with baking parchment.

Cook the popcorn according to the packet instructions. Remove any un-popped kernels and place the popped ones in the baking tin.

To make the caramel sauce, put the caster sugar in a medium saucepan and add 3 tablespoons of water. Place over low heat and stir to dissolve the sugar. Once the sugar has dissolved, increase the heat to medium-high and cook for 6–8 minutes, until the sugar has caramelised and turned a rich golden brown.

In a separate pan, heat the cream until it just comes to the boil. Carefully add the cream to the caramel (it will bubble!) along with the butter and salt, and whisk until combined. Pour the caramel sauce over the popcorn and mix to combine.

Melt the chocolate in a heatproof bowl over a saucepan of simmering water, making sure the water isn't touching the bottom of the bowl. Drizzle the melted chocolate over the popcorn and caramel and gently stir once to keep the chocolate and caramel slightly separate.

Flatten the popcorn mix with a greased hand and chill until set. Cut into eight bars when cool.

Makes: 8 bars
Preparation time: 5 minutes
Cooking time: 20 minutes

85g popcorn kernels
100g milk chocolate, broken into
    pieces

FOR THE SALTED CARAMEL
SAUCE
125g caster sugar
100ml double cream
30g butter, plus extra for greasing
½ tsp sea salt

My first experience of this treat was at school – the dinner ladies used to make huge trays of it. I hoped I would get the biggest slice as it was so good. If there was custard available I used to ladle that on top, too! I have finished this with a little smoked sea salt, which balances the sweetness of the caramel perfectly.

MILLIONAIRE'S SHORTBREAD

Preheat the oven to 200°C/180°C fan/gas 6. Grease a 20 × 30cm baking tin and line it with baking parchment.

To make the shortbread base, beat the sugar and butter together in a bowl until light and creamy. Mix in the flour until just combined. Flatten the dough into the lined baking tin using the back of a metal spoon then prick it all over with the prongs of a fork and chill for 20 minutes.

Once the shortbread has chilled, bake it for 20–25 minutes until just golden.

While the shortbread base is baking, make the caramel. Put the condensed milk, butter, sugar, golden syrup and table salt into a medium saucepan over medium heat. Stir continuously until the mixture begins to caramelise (this may take up to 25 minutes), reducing the heat slightly if it starts to bubble too vigorously. When it becomes thick and a rich golden colour, remove the pan from the heat, leave the caramel to cool for 5 minutes, then pour it over the top of the shortbread base and leave to cool completely.

Melt the chocolate in a bowl over a saucepan of simmering water, making sure the water doesn't touch the bottom of the bowl. Spread the melted chocolate over the top of the cooled caramel. Sprinkle with the smoked sea salt then chill for at least 3 hours before slicing it into 24 squares.

Makes: 24 squares
Preparation time: 10 minutes, plus
    3 hours 20 minutes chilling
Cooking time: around 30 minutes

200g milk or dark chocolate, broken
    into pieces
1–2 tsp smoked sea salt

FOR THE SHORTBREAD BASE
125g caster sugar
150g soft butter
220g plain flour

FOR THE CARAMEL
2 x 397g tins condensed milk
100g butter
100g soft dark brown sugar
4 tbsp golden syrup
½ tsp table salt

Lemon meringue pie is a delicious flavour combination, and here my twist on the classic is to layer it on sponge to make a tea-time delight. When selecting lemons at the supermarket, I always choose the brightest ones, and the least firm – this ensures they are the juiciest. I always avoid ambient lemon juice in bottles as it has a preservative in it that taints the natural flavour of the lemon and your recipes will never taste as good.

LEMON MERINGUE SLICE

Preheat the oven to 180°C/160°C fan/gas 4, grease a 20 × 30cm deep baking tin and line it with baking parchment.

To make the base, beat together the sugar and butter in a bowl until light and creamy, either by hand with an electric whisk or using a standmixer. Add the egg and mix well. Combine the baking powder with the flour and stir them into the mix until just combined. Press the dough into the baking tin to make an even layer and chill in the fridge for 20 minutes. Once chilled, bake for 15–20 minutes until just golden. Remove from the oven.

Grate the zest of 2 of the lemons into the granulated sugar, mix and set aside.

To make the filling, whisk the condensed milk in a bowl with the juice from the 4 lemons, the caster sugar and egg yolks until well combined. Pour the mixture over the pastry base in the tin and bake for 5 minutes, until just set but still a little wobbly in the centre. Remove from the oven and set aside while you make the meringue.

To make the meringue, whisk the egg whites in a spotlessly clean bowl with an electric whisk (or in a standmixer) on medium speed until they form stiff peaks. Increase the speed to high and gradually add the caster sugar, whisking continuously until you have a stiff meringue. Add the icing sugar and beat until just combined (the icing sugar makes the meringue softer).

Gently spread the meringue mixture over the lemon filling. Sprinkle the lemon zest and sugar mix over the top then bake for 10–15 minutes until crisp and golden. Remove from the oven and leave to cool before slicing and removing from the tin.

Serves: 12
Preparation time: 30 minutes,
    plus 20 minutes chilling
Cooking time: 40 minutes

2 tbsp granulated sugar

FOR THE BASE
125g caster sugar
150g soft butter
1 egg
1 tsp baking powder
250g plain flour

FOR THE LEMON FILLING
4 lemons
1 x 396g can condensed milk
125g caster sugar
4 egg yolks

FOR THE MERINGUE
3 egg whites
75g caster sugar
75g icing sugar, sifted

Freshly cooked, homemade doughnuts are pretty tough to beat, and adding rhubarb and custard to them makes this recipe even more moreish – a classic British combination for a reason. The zingy rhubarb works so well with the creamy custard. They do take a bit of work but are well worth the effort. Always eat the doughnuts fresh, on the day you make them. *See image on following pages.*

RHUBARB AND CUSTARD DOUGHNUTS

To make the rhubarb compote, put the ingredients in a medium saucepan and place over medium heat. Cook for about 7 minutes until the rhubarb is soft. Add a little more sugar if needed, then transfer to a container, cover and chill.

To make the custard, soak the gelatine leaves in a bowl of cold water for 5 minutes. Put the milk, cream and vanilla seeds in a saucepan and bring just to the boil, stirring frequently.

Put the egg yolks and sugar in a heatproof bowl and whisk until smooth. Slowly pour in the hot milk mixture, whisking continuously. Return the mixture back to the pan and cook over very low heat, stirring constantly, for about 5 minutes or until the custard coats the back of a wooden spoon. (Take care not to boil the custard as the egg yolks will scramble.) Squeeze the excess water from the gelatine and stir it into the hot custard until completely dissolved. Strain through a fine sieve into a clean container, cover and chill in the fridge.

To make the doughnut dough, place all ingredients except for the butter in the bowl of a standmixer fitted with a dough hook and mix until combined (alternatively, combine the ingredients in a mixing bowl with a wooden spoon). Knead the dough with your hands or using the dough hook and gradually add the butter. Knead for 5 minutes until smooth, then place the dough in an oiled bowl. Cover the bowl with lightly oiled clingfilm and leave in a warm place for 1–1½ hours, or until the dough has doubled in size.

When the dough has risen, turn it out of the bowl and divide it into four even-sized balls, then split each ball into two. With oiled hands, roll the eight balls until smooth and round. Place the balls, seam side down, on a lightly floured tray, gently cover with oiled clingfilm and leave in a warm place for 30 minutes.

Makes: 8
Preparation time: around 1 hour, plus chilling and 2 hours rising and proving
Cooking time: around 30 minutes

olive oil, for rolling the doughnuts
vegetable oil, for deep-frying and greasing

FOR THE RHUBARB COMPOTE
2 rhubarb stalks, trimmed and cut into 1cm lengths
50g caster sugar, plus extra if needed
1 tbsp grenadine

FOR THE VANILLA CUSTARD
2 gelatine leaves
150ml milk
150ml double cream
seeds from 1 vanilla pod
3 egg yolks
30g caster sugar

Combine the granulated sugar and cinnamon in a deep bowl.

Pour enough vegetable oil in a deep-fat fryer or large, deep saucepan to come up to 4–6cm and heat to 170°C. Once hot, carefully lower the doughnuts into the oil and fry for 4–5 minutes (in batches, if necessary – avoid overcrowding the pan), turning them with tongs until they are evenly deep golden and crisp. Remove from the oil with a slotted spoon, shake off any excess oil and roll them immediately in the cinnamon sugar.

Leave the doughnuts to cool then, using a knife, create a hole in one side. Wiggle the knife around carefully inside the doughnut, to create space for the rhubarb and custard.

Transfer the cooled rhubarb compote to a piping bag and pipe it into the eight doughnuts. Whisk the chilled custard until smooth then transfer it to a second piping bag and pipe it on top of the compote in the doughnuts.

FOR THE DOUGHNUT DOUGH

250g plain flour, plus extra for dusting
5g fast-action dried yeast or easy-bake yeast
75ml semi-skimmed or whole milk
2 medium eggs
pinch of table salt
50g soft unsalted butter

FOR THE CINNAMON SUGAR

4 tbsp granulated sugar
1 tsp ground cinnamon

This slice works well as an afternoon tea treat or as a pudding with a dollop of whipped cream. Soaking the prunes in the Earl Grey softens them as well as imparting a lovely flavour.

PRUNE AND WALNUT SLICE

To prepare the prunes, put 125ml of water, the sugar and tea bag in a small saucepan and bring to the boil. Put the prunes in a large heatproof bowl. Remove the tea bag from the pan and pour the liquid over the prunes into the bowl. Cover the bowl with clingfilm and store in a cool place for 2–3 days, turning the prunes every so often.

To make the pastry, mix the butter and sugar together in a bowl until just combined (you can do this with your hands or with a wooden spoon). Sift the flour, baking powder and table salt together then add half of the dry mixture to the butter and sugar and mix to form a smooth paste. Add the remaining flour and mix until fine crumbs are formed. Slowly add the cream, mixing just enough to bind to a dough. Shape the dough into a rectangle, wrap it in clingfilm and chill for 30 minutes.

Grease a 20 × 30cm baking tin and line it with baking parchment. Roll out the pastry on a floured surface to fit the baking tin. Take the pastry rectangle and gently place it in the baking tin, prick the base all over with the prongs of a fork and chill for a further 30 minutes.

Preheat the oven to 200°C/180°C fan/gas 6. Bake the pastry for 15 minutes.

While the pastry is baking, prepare the filling. Put the walnuts in a food processor and blitz until finely ground. Beat together the sugar and butter in a bowl by hand or in the bowl of a standmixer until light and creamy, then add the eggs, one at a time, beating well after each addition. Finally, add the pinch of sea salt and the ground walnuts and mix well. Cover the bowl with clingfilm and place in the fridge for 20 minutes.

Drain the prunes from the soaking liquid, reserving about 100ml.

Serves: 12
Preparation time: 30 minutes, plus
    2–3 days soaking and 1 hour
    20 minutes chilling
Cooking time: 1 hour

FOR THE PRUNES
50g caster sugar
1 Earl Grey tea bag
200g dried ready-to-eat prunes

FOR THE PASTRY
85g soft butter
115g caster sugar
225g plain flour, plus extra for
    dusting
1 tsp baking powder
½ tsp table salt
100ml double cream

FOR THE WALNUT FILLING
185g walnuts
150g caster sugar
150g soft butter
3 eggs
pinch of sea salt

Spread the walnut mix on the the baked pastry. Arrange the whole soaked prunes on top of the walnut mix. Bake for 45–50 minutes, until deep golden (covering the tin with foil for the final 10–15 minutes of baking time if it is getting too brown), and the walnut mix has just set in the centre. Remove from the oven and leave to cool for at least 15 minutes before brushing with the reserved prune soaking liquid.

This is a simple chocolate cake but with its shape, the beautiful shiny glaze and the sprinkling of gold dust, it ends up being something rather special. Bundt tins make for beautiful-looking cakes, whether you use a simple one or one of the more elaborate shapes. The trick with glaze is to pour it, not spread it, to create that mirror finish. The contrasting baked white-chocolate crumb finishes it beautifully.

CHOCOLATE CAKE WITH DARK CHOCOLATE GLAZE

Preheat the oven to 180°C/160°C fan/gas 4 and grease a 20cm Bundt tin (fluted cake ring) with butter.

Start by preparing the baked white-chocolate crumb. Put the white chocolate on a baking tray lined with baking parchment, or a silicone sheet. Bake for 20 minutes until dark brown, almost burnt-looking, stirring every 5 minutes. Remove from the oven and allow to cool.

When the baked white chocolate is cool, finely chop it to create a crumb.

Meanwhile, make the cake. Beat the butter and sugar in a bowl with an electric whisk or in the bowl of a standmixer for 5–7 minutes until light and creamy. Gradually add the egg yolks, beating well after each addition.

Melt the chocolate in a heatproof bowl set over a pan of simmering water (making sure the water doesn't touch the bottom of the bowl). Mix the melted chocolate, cocoa powder and the sea salt into the butter, sugar and egg yolks.

Add the flour and baking powder and mix until just combined. Add the buttermilk and stir to combine.

Whisk the egg whites in a separate spotlessly-clean bowl until they form soft peaks. Add a third of the whisked egg white to the chocolate and butter mixture and combine, to loosen it. Then gently fold in the remaining egg white using a large metal spoon.

Serves: 10
Preparation time: 20 minutes
Cooking time: 35 minutes, plus cooling

½ star anise, for grating

FOR THE BAKED WHITE-CHOCOLATE CRUMB
150g white chocolate, broken into pieces

FOR THE CAKE
175g soft butter, plus extra for greasing
175g soft light brown sugar
4 eggs, separated
175g dark chocolate (70% cocoa solids), broken into pieces
50g cocoa powder
1 tsp sea salt
175g plain flour
1 tsp baking powder
50ml buttermilk

Transfer the cake batter to the prepared tin and bake for around 35 minutes, until the cake is just firm in the centre and a skewer comes out clean when inserted into the middle. Remove from the oven and allow to cool in the tin for 15 minutes, then turn out onto a wire rack and leave to cool completely.

To make the glaze, put the pieces of chocolate in a heatproof bowl. Heat the cream in a small saucepan until it reaches boiling point then pour it over the chocolate. Put the sugar and cocoa powder in the same saucepan and add 100ml water. Bring to a gentle simmer for 2 minutes, whisking well, then strain through a fine sieve onto the chocolate mix and whisk until smooth.

Line your work surface with a double layer of clingfilm.

Place the cake on top of the clingfilm, top side down. Gradually drizzle the glaze over the cake, to coat it evenly, and chill until set.

Once the glaze has set, liberally sprinkle the baked white-chocolate crumb over the top of the cake. Grate the star anise over the top of the crumb and cake using a Microplane grater.

FOR THE DARK CHOCOLATE GLAZE
120g dark chocolate (70% cocoa solids), broken into pieces
80ml whipping cream
2 tbsp caster sugar
1 tbsp cocoa powder

Coffee and walnut cake is a classic English bake. I have slightly enhanced the traditional version so it could be a dessert as well as an afternoon tea offering. Use espresso if possible or, if not, use a strong coffee.

ESPRESSO, WHITE CHOCOLATE AND WALNUT CAKE

Preheat the oven to 180°C/160°C fan/gas 4, grease the bases of two 20cm cake tins and line with baking parchment.

Put the 25g sugar in a bowl and add 25ml boiling water and stir until the sugar dissolves. Coat the walnuts in the sugar solution, sprinkle them with the salt then spread them out on a baking tray and bake for 10–15 minutes, until golden. Remove from the oven, leave to cool then finely chop.

To make the cake, beat the butter and sugar together in a bowl for 5–7 minutes until light and fluffy. Add the eggs, one at a time, beating well after each addition and scraping down the sides of the bowl.

Sift the flour, baking powder and salt together. Add a third of the flour to the butter mixture and beat well. Add half the espresso, beat well, then add another third of the flour and beat until fully combined. Add the remaining espresso and final third of the flour, beating well.

Divide the cake batter evenly between the prepared tins and bake for 20–25 minutes, until the cakes are just firm in the centre and a skewer inserted into the middle of each one comes out clean. Remove from the oven and leave the cakes to cool in the tins.

To make the espresso mascarpone, dissolve the sugar in the warm espresso, leave to cool, then whisk it into the mascarpone.

Spread the espresso mascarpone onto the top of one of the cakes. Place the other cake on top of the espresso mascarpone.

Serves: 8–10
Preparation time: 25 minutes
Cooking time: 50 minutes, plus cooling

25g caster sugar
100g walnuts
¼ tsp table salt

FOR THE CAKE
200g soft butter, plus extra for greasing
200g light muscovado sugar
4 eggs
200g self-raising flour
1 tsp baking powder
pinch of table salt
65ml espresso, cooled

FOR THE ESPRESSO MASCARPONE
25g caster sugar
50ml warm espresso
150g mascarpone

To make the icing, melt the white chocolate in a heatproof
bowl over a saucepan of simmering water, making sure the
water doesn't touch the bottom of the bowl, then allow to cool
slightly. Beat the butter and icing sugar together in a bowl
until light and fluffy and add the melted white chocolate.
Pipe or spread the icing onto the top and sides of the cake,
then sprinkle liberally with the chopped, candied walnuts.

FOR THE WHITE
CHOCOLATE ICING
150g white chocolate,
    broken into pieces
150g soft butter
150g icing sugar

Pink grapefruit has a wonderfully aromatic flavour. The flesh also has a beautiful pink colour and looks great in desserts, the grapefruit curd enhances the overall flavour of the cake. Serve as a dessert, or for afternoon tea.

PINK GRAPEFRUIT SPONGE

Combine a quarter of the grapefruit zest with the granulated sugar in a bowl. Mix well, spread out onto baking parchment and leave somewhere warm to dry out.

To make the grapefruit curd, put 80ml of grapefruit juice, another quarter of the grapefruit zest, the caster sugar, egg yolks and egg in a medium heatproof bowl and set the bowl over a saucepan of gently simmering water, making sure the water doesn't touch the bottom of the bowl. Whisk constantly until the mix is light and fluffy and begins to thicken to the consistency of custard. This will take about 10 minutes.

Remove the saucepan from the heat, with the bowl of curd on top, and whisk in the butter, cube by cube, until it is all incorporated. Pass the curd through a fine sieve into a bowl, cover the surface of the curd with clingfilm (to prevent a skin forming) and chill.

Preheat the oven to 170°C/150°C fan/gas 4. Grease two 20cm cake tins and line the bases with baking parchment.

To make the sponge, put the eggs and caster sugar in a heatproof bowl set over a saucepan of simmering water, making sure the water doesn't touch the bottom of the bowl, and whisk until the mixture reaches approximately 45°C on a sugar thermometer.

Transfer the egg and sugar mix to a standmixer, or use an electric whisk, and whisk for 10 minutes until light and fluffy. Gently fold the sifted flour into the egg mix, until just combined. Add the remaining grapefruit zest to the melted butter and gradually add the butter to the sponge mix.

Divide the sponge mix between the prepared cake tins and bake for 10–15 minutes until lightly golden and firm to touch. Remove the tins from

Serves: 8
Preparation time: 30 minutes, plus chilling and cooling
Cooking time: around 25 minutes

grated zest and juice of 2 pink grapefruits (around 340ml juice in total)
2 tbsp granulated sugar
2 tbsp caster sugar
150ml double cream

FOR THE GRAPEFRUIT CURD
50g caster sugar
1 egg, plus 2 egg yolks
80g soft butter, diced

FOR THE SPONGE
4 eggs
150g caster sugar
175g plain flour, sifted
75g butter, melted, plus extra for greasing

the oven and allow the cakes to cool for 30 minutes before removing them from the tins. Leave to cool right side up on a wire rack.

Heat the remaining grapefruit juice in a pan with the 2 tablespoons of caster sugar over low heat until the sugar has dissolved. Increase the heat and let it bubble away for 5–7 minutes until you have 100ml of syrup left. Drizzle the syrup over the top of both the sponge cakes and sprinkle one of the cakes with the grapefruit sugar.

Whisk the double cream in a bowl until it forms soft peaks. Spread the top of the sponge which doesn't have the grapefruit sugar with the grapefruit curd. Top with the whipped cream. Place the grapefruit-sugar covered sponge on top of the cream.

Rosemary is a fantastic herb to use in sweet baking and desserts. Its flavour and aroma enhance most sweet things and this cake proves that point. Pears are available all year round but the seasons when you will find they are much juicier are autumn and winter.

PEAR, ALMOND AND ROSEMARY CAKE

Preheat the oven to 180°C/160°C fan/gas 4, grease the base of a 23cm loose-bottomed cake tin and line it with baking parchment.

Peel the pears. Halve one lengthways and remove the core. Cut it into fine 2mm-thick slices and lay the slices on the bottom of the cake tin in a spiral shape. Coarsely grate the other two pears and set them aside.

Beat the butter and sugar in a bowl with an electric whisk or in the bowl of a standmixer until light and fluffy. Add the eggs one at a time, beating well after each one is added, then add the grated pear and mix well.

Once smooth, add the flour, salt, ground almonds and two-thirds of the rosemary and gently fold together until combined. Gently spoon the cake batter into the tin, over the pears, and smooth the top.

Bake for 30–35 minutes, until the cake is just firm in the centre and a skewer inserted into the middle of the cake comes out clean. Remove from the oven and allow to cool slightly, then carefully remove the cake from the tin and flip it over so it's sitting on a wire rack pear side up. Brush the warm cake with the honey and sprinkle with the remaining rosemary.

Serves: 10–12
Preparation time: 15 minutes
Cooking time: 35 minutes

150g soft butter, plus extra for greasing
3 ripe pears
150g caster sugar
3 eggs
200g self-raising flour
pinch of salt
100g ground almonds
2 tbsp chopped rosemary needles
2 tbsp runny honey

CONVERSION CHARTS

DRY WEIGHTS

METRIC	IMPERIAL	METRIC	IMPERIAL
5g	¼oz	400g	14oz
8/10g	⅓oz	425g	15oz
15g	½oz	450g	1lb
20g	¾oz	475g	1lb 1oz
25g	1oz	500g	1lb 2oz
30/35g	1¼oz	550g	1lb 3oz
40g	1½oz	600g	1lb 5oz
50g	2oz	625g	1lb 6oz
60/70g	2½oz	650g	1lb 7oz
75/85/90g	3oz	675g	1½lb
100g	3½oz	700g	1lb 9oz
110/120g	4oz	750g	1lb 10oz
125/130g	4½oz	800g	1¾lb
135/140/150g	5oz	850g	1lb 14oz
170/175g	6oz	900g	2lb
200g	7oz	950g	2lb 2oz
225g	8oz	1kg	2lb 3oz
250g	9oz	1.1kg	2lb 6oz
265g	9½oz	1.25kg	2¾lb
275g	10oz	1.3/1.4kg	3lb
300g	11oz	1.5kg	3lb 5oz
325g	11½oz	1.75/1.8kg	4lb
350g	12oz	2kg	4lb 4oz
375g	13oz		

568ml = 1 UK pint (20fl oz) | 16fl oz = 1 US pint

LIQUID MEASURES

METRIC	IMPERIAL (US)	CUPS
15ml	½fl oz	1 tbsp
20ml	¾fl oz	
30ml	1fl oz	⅛ cup
60ml	2fl oz	¼ cup
75ml	2½fl oz	
90ml	3fl oz	⅓ cup
100ml	3½fl oz	
120ml	4fl oz	½ cup
135ml	4½fl oz	
160ml	5fl oz	⅔ cup
180ml	6fl oz	¾ cup
210ml	7fl oz	
240ml	8fl oz	1 cup
265ml	9fl oz	
300ml	10fl oz	1¼ cups
350ml	12fl oz	1½ cups
415ml	14fl oz	
480ml	16fl oz / 1 pint	2 cups
530ml	18fl oz	2¼ cups
1 litre	32fl oz	4 cups

OVEN TEMPERATURES

°C	°F	GAS MARK	DESCRIPTION
110	225	¼	cool
120	250	½	cool
140	275	1	very low
150	300	2	very low
160	325	3	low to moderate
170/180	350	4	moderate
190	375	5	moderately hot
200	400	6	hot
210/220	425	7	hot
230/240	450	8	hot

INDEX

ACKNOWLEDGEMENTS

Books start as a collection of ideas on paper, working their way to recipe concepts, then through to actual recipes. Seeing it all come to life, from inception to the photo shoots, then from the proofs to the finished book is rather remarkable. And, it's only possible through a solid bunch of people contributing in many different ways.

First of all I would like to thank Chantelle Nicholson as my co-author. Her commitment to the restaurants – and the company – is the reason we are here today. This is her fifth book with me over 14 years, and it has been an amazing journey. Thank you.

I would also like to thank Grace Cheetham, for believing in me and both *Marcus at Home* and *New Classics*. Your vision, guidance and commitment have been inspirational. Thank you to my agent Rosemary Scoular from United Agents for her support and direction.

A very big thank you to the teams in my restaurants: Marcus, The Gilbert Scott and Tredwells. I feel very lucky to be surrounded by such talented, creative and thoughtful individuals who deliver so much 365 days a year, and who also make projects such as this possible.

Jonathan Gregson, you are a true professional, and a gentleman! You make the food sing on camera. Marina Filippelli, your vision in your food styling and your kitchen humour (!) are beyond wonderful. Becks Wilkinson, your styling and support really shone through in this book. Sarah Hammond, your military precision and organisation are a wonder to behold – thank you for making the whole process seamless and enjoyable.

James Empringham, aka Jim, you always manage to make me laugh at the right time. Your vision and eye for detail are exceptional. Jo Harris, your prop styling is impeccably on point and makes everything come together so well.

A big thank you to our suppliers, who also ensured we had the very best produce for the shoot. Natoora: wonderful fresh produce and Italian goods *www.natoora.co.uk*; Daily Fish Supplies: fresh seafood and fish *www.dailyfishsupplies.com*; HG Walter: butcher *www.hgwalter.com*; and, to one of my favourite clothing and footwear makers, Oliver Sweeney, for the great stuff provided for the shoot *www.oliversweeney.com*.

And to finish on a slight cliché, teamwork really does make the dream work. Thank you to everyone else involved at various stages – I hope you love the book as much as I do.